ANCIENT CHINA

ANCIENT CHINA

The discoveries of post-Liberation
Chinese archaeology by

WILLIAM WATSON

with an introduction
by Magnus Magnusson

New York Graphic Society

International Standard Book
Number 0–8212–0608–7
Library of Congress Catalog Card
Number 73–91129
First published in Great Britain 1974
by the British Broadcasting
Corporation, London.
Published in the United States of
America 1974 by
New York Graphic Society,
Greenwich, Connecticut 06830.
Printed in England

Contents

Introduction 7

1 Lan-t'ien Man, Peking Man
and their Successors 15

2 Neolithic 23

3 The Bronze Age 35

4 The Han Empire 55

5 The T'ang Dynasty 77

6 The Sung Dynasty 95

7 The Yüan Dynasty 101

Thanks are due as follows for permission to reproduce illustrations (colour plates are referred to in Roman numerals): The Institute of Archaeology, Peking: I–IX, 1–4, 13, 15, 17, 18, 27–9, 33, 34, 36, 38, 40, 53, 57–62, 65, 66, 68–70, 72–6, 84, 85; Benaki Museum, Athens: 51, 52, 56; Trustees of the British Museum: 16, 22, 25, 43, 44, 50; Freer Gallery of Art, Washington: 23, 45.

The photographs used for 46–8, 55, 78 were the work of Werner Forman; Robert Harding supplied pictures for 8, 13, 15, 27, 28, 32, 33, 35, 40, 53, 59, 60, 66, 68, 70, I–IX; and George Rainbird Ltd for 1, 72, 73. The maps and diagrams were drawn by Hugh Ribbans.

The author's particular thanks go to Mr Peter Campbell for his constant care and help in designing the book and selecting the illustrations.

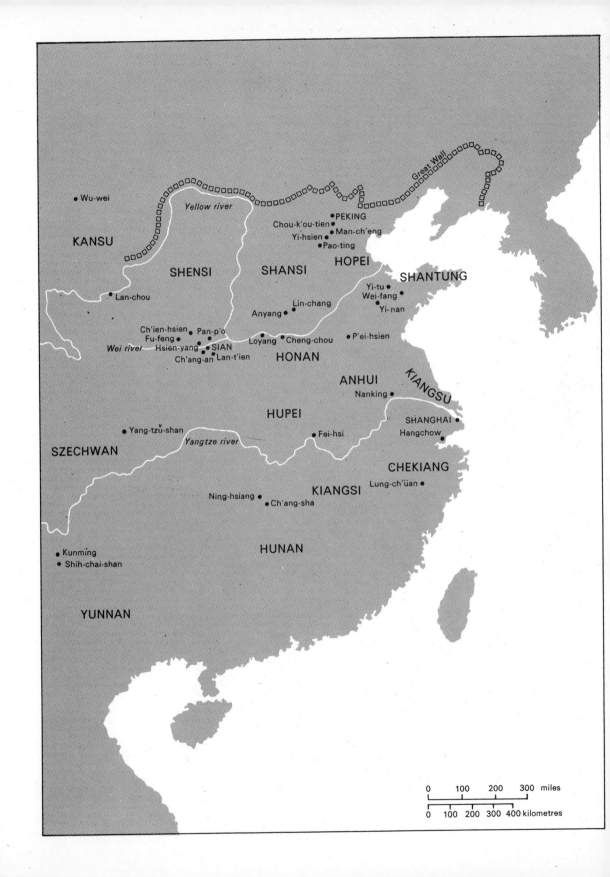

Wu-wei

Yellow river

KANSU

SHENSI

SHANSI

HOPEI

Great Wall

Chou-k'ou-tien • PEKING
Yi-hsien • Man-ch'eng
• Pao-ting

SHANTUNG

Lan-chou

Yi-tu •
Wei-fang •
Yi-nan •

Anyang • Lin-chang

Ch'ien-hsien • Pan-p'o
Fu-feng •
Hsien-yang • SIAN
Wei river
Ch'ang-an Lan-t'ien

Loyang • Cheng-chou
P'ei-hsien •

HONAN

ANHUI

KIANGSU

Nanking •

HUPEI

SHANGHAI
Hangchow

Yang-tzǔ-shan •

Fei-hsi •

Yangtze river

SZECHWAN

CHEKIANG

Lung-ch'üan •

KIANGSI

Ning-hsiang •
• Ch'ang-sha

HUNAN

Kunming •
Shih-chai-shan •

YUNNAN

0   100   200   300 miles

0   100 200 300 400 kilometres

Introduction

This book is the outcome of a pilgrimage to China I made on behalf of the BBC with Professor William Watson of the University of London. Professor Watson went as an acknowledged authority on Chinese art and archaeology; I went as a novice. It was my first visit to China, his third.

But we both went there to learn: to learn about the advances that have been made in recent years in exploring China's past, and to report on them in two film documentaries that were being produced by Michael Gill. Our reports were designed to coincide with the magnificent exhibition of Chinese archaeological treasures at The Royal Academy in London – the first major display to come to Europe from China for nearly forty years. And our brief was to give these treasures of ancient China a context in the new China of today.

It was an unforgettable journey: a journey down the glittering centuries of China's imperial history, across the endless vistas of this huge land that houses a quarter of mankind. China makes an overwhelming impression on the visitor, of sheer size and numbers. Some 800 million people in a country the size of Canada, and curiously *nice* people, too. I use the word advisedly, because in the west we have so many ingrained prejudices about the Yellow Peril and all that sort of nonsense. The Chinese people we met were earnest, friendly, dedicated, and essentially nice. Compared with westerners they are almost puritanical in their way of

life, devoted to the ideals of revolution – the Communist Liberation of 1949 – in rather the same way as the Puritans of Cromwell's England must have been. There is no crime in China, for instance; no theft, no pickpockets. There is no poverty in China; everyone is enabled to buy, very cheaply, sufficient food to live on and two sets of uniform blue or grey clothing a year. There are no beggars in China. There is no disease in China, no flies – indeed, the Chinese are fanatically concerned with health, and can boast one of the finest health services in the world.

That doesn't make it paradise, at least to a European. To the western eye, attuned to the lurid commercialism of urban life, the cities of China, even Peking, appear drab and dusty by comparison. Instead of neon-lit hoardings there are only great posters proclaiming a thought by Chairman Mao, a revolutionary exhortation. Instead of streets jammed with cars, there are streets teeming with bicycles. There are no privately-owned cars in China, only official cars, and everyone goes by bike. Instead of frantic pace and pressure, there are crocodiles of schoolchildren marching to school singing appropriate revolutionary songs.

There's a uniformity that the westerner finds depressing. It's a little sad that this great nation that invented the art of writing and printing books should today print only 'official' books. Freedom of expression has been suppressed, and there is no point in trying to blink the fact. Perhaps it is the only way in which the much-needed Revolution could have succeeded, but it is a little saddening.

Even so, it forces you to re-examine your own standards and values – a bit uncomfortably, too. In fact, I think the most illuminating remark I heard during our visit was the day we left China and reached Hong Kong. I was all for dumping our luggage where we stood in order to go and buy something, but Professor Watson said, 'Wait a minute, you can't just leave that stuff lying there – you're not in China now, you know.' It was a sobering reminder of the difference between our civilisations.

It was impossible to be unaware of this immensely different background as we travelled across China, from Peking up to the Great Wall, then by delightful steam train down to Canton in the south.

Archaeology in China is a relatively young science. The first excavations weren't made until the 1920s, fifty years after Heinrich Schliemann had begun to open up the history of the Mycenean civilisation of Greece. In China the first excavations were amateur and tentative; but early in the thirties an official Academia Sinica was formed to undertake serious, systematic excavation. It had some conspicuous successes during its short life. The earliest stages of Chinese civilisation began to emerge from the soil – most notably the discovery of Peking Man, the revelation of a Chinese Neolithic stage that no one had suspected

existed (c. 6000 BC onwards), and startling confirmation of a magnificent Bronze Age dynasty, the Shang (c. 1600–1000 BC) whose lost capital, at An-yang, was systematically excavated.

All this immensely promising and rewarding work came to an end in the mid-1930s when Japan invaded China. The next ten years were a desperate battle for survival as the Chinese fought the invaders and fought amongst themselves. It was not until the victory of Chairman Mao and the foundation of the People's Republic of China in 1949 that archaeology could come into its own again. The Academy of Sciences was re-formed with a special archaeological division.

The defeated Chiang Kai-Chek had taken all the cultural treasures of ancient China with him on his flight, and the most spectacular discovery of all – the fossilised remains of Peking Man, the discovery that had electrified the world before the war – had unaccountably disappeared; it had been dispatched for safe-keeping in the direction of America, but became a war casualty somewhere on the way.

And so, in 1949, Chinese archaeology had to start again. And it is the achievements of post-Liberation Chinese archaeology that were celebrated in the Royal Academy exhibition. The revolutionary republic was and is closely concerned with the education of its people; education in China has always been regarded in terms of the past, in terms of a close attention to historical and cultural traditions. In the new China, this attitude is well summed up by Chairman Mao's celebrated dictum, 'Let the past serve the present'. Antiquarianism in China has a long and honourable history; now, after 1949, it was being scientifically brought up to date, using the techniques of archaeology pioneered in the west. Then, in 1966, it all stopped, or at least it all seemed to stop. The Cultural Revolution burgeoned, and for six years China was silent.

The learned journals in China only restarted publication in 1972; but it quickly became clear that, far from an orgy of destruction under the Red Guards as had been feared, there had been an intense amount of creative work during those silent years. Chinese archaeologists had been hard at work, and they had been ably supported by what the publications refer to as 'the peasants, workers, and members of the Liberation Army'. The anger about the imperial past had spilled over into threatening demonstrations against some imperial sites and treasures, but it had steadied and been channelled into a more constructive attitude: that the treasures of the past demonstrated the ageless skill and genius of the working class who had made them, not the genius of the emperors who had enjoyed them.

The history of China is a bewildering kaleidoscope of dynasties and wars, of weirdly unspellable people and places. In this book, Professor Watson puts it all into authoritative perspec-tive, as he did for me as we travelled together through the past into the present. Let me highlight some of the impressions I garnered.

Panp'o is the most spectacular neolithic site that has been excavated anywhere in Asia, perhaps anywhere in the world. We went there right at the start of our journey, because it comes right at the start of China. Panp'o was a village settlement of New Stone Age people; radiocarbon dates suggest that it was first occupied around 5000 BC. It lies in the suburbs of the textile-manufacturing city of Sian (population 2,500,000), the capital of Shensi province in north-central China. It was discovered in 1953 when foundations were being dug for a new factory.

Today it is one of the major showpieces of Chinese archaeology, and with good reason. The excavated site has been roofed over to shelter it from the elements, and visitors can walk on raised passageways round a landscape of sculpted floors and pits and postholes. Archaeology is basically just a hole in the ground; but at Panp'o the hole has been brilliantly interpreted in visual terms, to recreate the sort of life led by these early Chinese farmers. Four museum pavilions tell the story of the site lucidly and vividly; and a reconstructed hut, based on the shadowy evidence unearthed by the archaeologists, allows you to feel precisely what it was like to live in those times; to handle the fine pottery made in the village, to see in the mind's eye the activities of planting and harvesting, fishing and hunting, that went on there. All too often, archaeology seems to be about the dead, because only the dead care about eternity; at Panp'o, you meet the living.

Shang, Chou, Ch'in, Han, Ch'i, Wei, Sui, T'ang – the dynasties of China reel past the untutored mind. In the end, for self-preservation's sake, I decided to cling to only three – Ch'in, Han, and T'ang. The Ch'in was a short-lived dynasty, from 221–207 BC, but it had two claims to significance in my mind. In the first place, it was the name from which, by some quirk of history, the name China derives. And secondly, it was the first Ch'in emperor who, around 220 BC, more than three centuries before Hadrian built a wall across north Britain, joined up the various frontier walls in the north of China to create the Great Wall. Hadrian's Wall is contemptibly puny beside the Great Wall of China – a mere seventy miles as against nearly 3000 miles. The Great Wall must be one of the most staggering projects on earth, snaking and winding up and down the mountains like a monstrous stone serpent. It took 300,000 men ten years to complete; and it's the only building on earth, so it's said, that is visible from the moon.

The Ch'in didn't last long; in 206 BC they were overthrown by the founder of one of China's most glorious dynasties. The Han lasted, with a brief interruption, from 206 BC to AD 220, straddling the crucial era of Christian and Roman Europe.

Two marvellous archaeological phenomena have come from the Han dynasty: the jade suits of Man-ch'eng, and the 'Flying Horse' of Mr Chang. The jade suits were discovered in two tombs in Hopei Province in 1968. They were the burial robes of Liu Sheng and his wife, Tou Wan, prince and princess of Chungshan, close kinsmen of the Emperor himself. They had failed in their primary purpose of keeping the bodies from decaying – nothing was left of Liu Sheng but a few teeth. But they represent all the immemorial, matchless skill of Chinese craftsmen down the ages, working at a time when thousands of their fellows were dying of famine – and Liu Sheng, noted lecher and drunkard, was dying of luxury.

The 'Flying Horse' of the Han period is surely destined to become one of the world's most celebrated sculptures. It is a perfect representation of a horse at full speed, balancing on one hoof (a remarkable technical feat in itself) on the back of a swallow surprised in flight. During the Han dynasty the Chinese were obsessed with the need for good horses for their cavalry – not the pony-sized steeds of the northern nomads who harassed them, but the great big 'Celestial Horses' of the west, from Afghanistan. One emperor led a vast expedition 2000 miles to capture them; he succeeded, but only at the cost of nearly four-fifths of his army. Mr Chang, the occupant of the tomb from which the 'Flying Horse' came, was clearly just as appreciative of good horse-flesh – and even better art.

Finally, I come to the T'ang. This was the Golden Age of China, symbolised again by horses, the magnificent pottery horses of the T'ang tombs. It lasted from AD 618 to 906, the period when Europe moved out of the Dark Ages, through Charlemagne into the robust centuries of Viking expansion. What brought the T'ang period most to life for me was a visit we made to the tomb of the Princess Yung-T'ai. It stands in the middle of a royal burial field on the plains to the north of the city of Sian – China's equivalent of Egypt's Valley of the Kings. It was here that T'ang royalty and their high-ranking officials were buried, in deep subterranean chambers piled with flat-topped pyramids.

Princess Yung-T'ai died at the age of 17 in the year 701. She was the grand-daughter of one of the most formidable old dragons ever to occupy the Dragon Throne of China – the Empress Wu, who ruled the empire with an iron, unrelenting hand in the last decades of the seventh century. A palace informer told her that her grand-daughter, Yung-T'ai, and her brother, had been heard whispering criticisms of the government; and the old Empress instantly demanded that Yung-T'ai and her brother should commit suicide. Which they did.

Yung-T'ai was newly married at the time, to a commander of the Second Rank of Imperial Carriages. And, as it turned out, her death was a terrible

mistake. The informer had got it wrong. Her tomb was excavated in 1960, and Professor Watson and I were the first Europeans to be invited to see it. As we walked down the sloping passage towards the tomb-chamber itself, past walls vividly painted with animated court-scenes, past wall-niches crammed with glorious T'ang pottery, I found myself thinking irresistibly of the tomb of Tutankhamun. For Yung-T'ai's tomb, like Tutankhamun's, had been looted by tomb robbers soon after the burial.

The evidence was there to see when the archaeologists first came on the scene. A soil survey round the pyramid revealed that someone had sunk a shaft into the ground near the base of the tomb. The archaeologists followed it, digging their way down just as the intruders had done. The shaft brought them into the underground passage near the ante-chamber of the tomb itself. But at the bottom of the shaft they found a macabre sight – a skeleton lying on top of a heap of gold and jade and silver, his skull split open, and an iron axe-head nearby. The thieves had fallen out when the robbery was completed; perhaps the last man in had been an informer, whose value to the gang was now over. He was left to share the centuries of solitude with the little princess who had been falsely accused of treason.

It is stories like these, stories of terror and tragedy, that bring Chinese history to spectacular life for the layman. Imperial China was a place of emperors and dragons and concubines. When you visit the Forbidden City in Peking, the great palace complex created by Kublai Khan, grandson of Genghis Khan, one tends to remember the love-stories that took place there rather than the wickedness of despotism. The emperors, after all, were human. They lived, and they loved: they loved life, and poetry, and the arts, as intensely and passionately as sometimes they loved their women.

Sir Mortimer Wheeler once wrote about archaeology that its business was to dig up people, not things. It is the people of ancient China that entrance the mind; it is the people that Chinese archaeology has brought to life again, with whatever disapproval of the sort of people they were.

MAGNUS MAGNUSSON

Chronological Table

Palaeolithic period:	about 600,000–7000 BC
Neolithic period:	about 7000–1600 BC
Shang dynasty:	about 1600–1027 BC
Western Chou dynasty:	1027–771 BC
Period of the Spring and Autumn Annals:	770–475 BC
Technology	
Period of the Warring States:	475–221 BC
Ch'in dynasty:	221–207 BC
Western Han dynasty:	206 BC–AD 8
Kingdom of Tien	about 3rd century BC–1st century AD
Hsin dynasty (Wang Mang)	AD 8–23
Eastern Han dynasty	AD 24–220
Period of the Six dynasties	AD 220–590
Central Asia, Han to T'ang dynasties	1st century BC–8th century AD
Sui dynasty	AD 581–618
T'ang dynasty	AD 618–906
Five dynasties	AD 907–960
Sung dynasty	AD 960–1279
Liao dynasty	AD 916–1125
Chin dynasty	AD 1115–1234
Yuan dynasty	AD 1271–1368

Cast of the skull and lower jaw-bone of the ape-man found at Lan-t'ien, Shensi. The remains are dated geologically to a time about 600,000 years ago. The reconstruction shows eye orbits of unusually flattened shape. The projection of the eyebrow ridge is very pronounced (see also fig. 3) and· the low forehead indicates small cranial capacity.

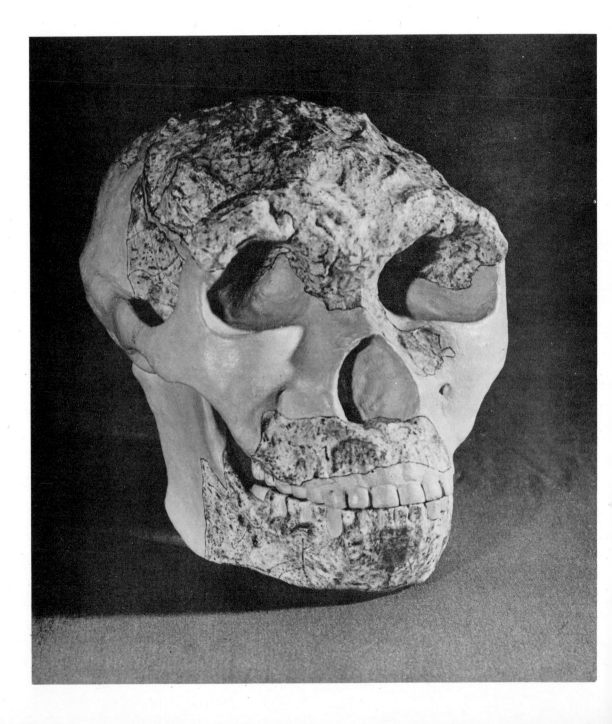

I

Lan-t'ien Man, Peking Man
and their successors

For fifty years it has been known that half a million years ago, at a time corresponding to the middle period of the Ice Age as it was experienced in Europe and northern America, an early species of man inhabited China. The first discovery was of primitive human skulls in the rubble filling fissures in limestone cliffs being quarried at Chou-k'ou-tien, about 25 miles south-west of Peking. The skulls were associated with the broken bones of animals – evidently food refuse – and with stone implements, proving that they belonged to a toolmaker and were, therefore, human. Yet physically he resembled, in some respects, the anthropoid apes. The skull has only about two-thirds of the modern capacity, with a low forehead and a jutting jaw, but fleeting chin. The heavy eyebrow ridge is the most noticeable feature. His height – about five feet – would not be unusual in China even today, and his high cheek-bones and broad nose are perennial characteristics of the East Asian races. The bones of about forty-five individuals were found at Chou-k'ou-tien. They include both sexes and fifteen children; it was the first time that any indication had been found of the family life of palaeolithic man. Even more decisive indications of purely human activity were traces of fire. As a tool-making, fire-making creature, Peking Man (*Sinanthropus pekinensis*) was established as one of the earliest members of the human family.[1]

But before hearing more of his habits

one should notice that he was not the first known type of man in China. Excavations carried out under supervision in Shensi province produced evidence of a slightly more primitive hominid. At Ch'en-chia-wo village in the Lan-t'ien district a human lower jaw was found in 1963, and the following year, at Kung-wang-ling in the same district, a skull-cap, parts of the lateral skull bones and parts of right and left upper jaws, with two molars in position, came to light. The bones are highly and similarly fossilised, and so are believed to belong to the same period and the same sub-species. (Different sub-species of palaeolithic man have not been found in close association.) Some deductions can be made from a study of the skull fragments, and the head, neck and shoulders reconstructed (fig. 1).

The wear of the molars suggests the age: if they belonged to a modern northern Chinese it would be about forty, but the wearing of the teeth of the fossil hominid would be more rapid and the individual is therefore likely to be nearer thirty years old. Judging from the size of the teeth the skull bones appear to belong to a female, though this cannot be quite certain. The morphological features of the skull have the same general character as Peking Man, *Sinanthropus pekin-*

---

[1]The skulls found at Chou-k'ou-tien in 1928 were lost during the Second World War; but since 1966 another skull and several long bones of Peking Man have been recovered in systematic excavation.

ensis, and the Ape Man, *Pithecanthropus,* known from bones found early in this century in the Trinil beds of east Java. The formation of the eye sockets is even more primitive than that of these two related species of men. The eyebrow ridge is long and heavy, forming a continuous bar, and the eye orbits tend to a rectangular outline, the roof of the orbit being particularly flat, and the depression of the tear-gland missing. The forehead is very low and receding, and the outer ends of the eyebrow ridge project even more sideways than is the case in Peking and Java Man. One distinct character of the Lan-t'ien skull is the extraordinary thickness of the cranial wall, which is the greatest seen among the hominids of the period: it is approximately half as thick again as the skull of Peking Man, and nearly twice the thickness of a modern human skull.

The brain capacity of Lan-t'ien Man is estimated as 780 cc, close to that of Peking Man. The conclusion is that the sub-species he represents is more primitive than that of Chou-k'ou-tien and the Ape Man of Java from the Trinil beds. But he is paralleled approximately by another Java type, the *Pithecanthropus robustus* of the Djetis beds. The geological history of the last million years in East Asia cannot yet be matched exactly with the sequence of geological and climatic events in the West, and therefore close comparison of the physical and cultural evolution of man at the two ends of Asia is not possible. But in broad terms the earliest men in China were living at the same time as the second great interglacial age in Europe.

As much as a hundred thousand years may separate Lan-t'ien Man from his follower, Peking Man. The most important observation so far as China is concerned is that both lived *before* the deposition of the loess, the yellow earth, had begun in north-west China. This fact serves to distinguish the early horizon of hominids from the period when modern man, *Homo sapiens,* made his appearance in east Asia, for the latter was present in China *during* the formation of the yellow earth. It was on this fertile soil that the first farming communities were destined to flourish many millennia later.

The climate in which Lan-t'ien Man lived was probably not much different from that which prevailed at the time of Peking Man. It can be broadly judged from the animals that were his contemporaries. They suggest well-wooded but not jungle terrain, with much open grassland and dense brushwood. (The numerous small rodents vouch for the latter.) Horse, gazelle, hare, deer and a small wild ox point to grasslands; the rhinoceros and some species of deer suggest comparative abundance of water (probably in ponds and marshes such as are rare in the region today); bear, porcupine and wild boar would seem to require woodland glades as their habitat. All of this may suggest a climate rather more equable than that of inland China at the present time, with an average temperature somewhat higher, but not reaching the extreme of the tropical interludes experienced in the inter-glacials of Europe. The grassland and woodland species were preyed on by the carnivores: hyena, panther and lion.

To this fauna the collection of animals recognised from Chou-k'ou-tien adds the sabre-toothed tiger (a denizen also of the Thames valley in its time and no doubt as resistant to very varied climates as the modern tiger). Statistics of the numbers of animal species show that both the Lan-t'ien and the Chou-k'ou-tien deposits belong to the middle (Pleistocene) period of the ice age, but the difference between the two sites points to fairly rapid change in the animal population of central China in this period. Thus of the fossil mammals found at Lan-t'ien only sixty per cent were present at Chou-k'ou-tien, while four species known to Lan-t'ien Man had apparently become extinct before the appearance of Peking Man. At Lan-t'ien only 37 per cent of the animals represent species which survive in the region today.

The stone tools made by Lan-t'ien Man correspond to those of the Middle Acheulian culture of France and southern England. Since only vein-quartz and quartzite were available, and not the cleanly-breaking flint of Europe, the Chinese tools look coarser in comparison. The smaller tools consist of squarish flakes struck off larger pieces of the stone, and contrived to

yield a fairly straight cutting edge. Presumably some initial flaking of the parent lump took place, in order to determine more or less the shape of the desired flake. The flakes might then be retouched to thin down the back or refine the edge. All of this process presupposes a degree of fore-thought which must already be a considerable advance on the methods of the first human tool-makers. The larger instrument is a heavy point some seven inches long, tapering from a butt three and a half inches wide. The form is that of the classic hand-axe of palaeolithic man in Europe, such as is found frequently in the lower gravels of the lower Thames valley, and although in the Chinese specimen the flaking is less regular, as enforced by the inferior material, it is nonetheless carefully controlled.

The number of Lan-t'ien Man's tools that were found is not sufficient for any final conclusions on his manual skill, but Peking Man has left behind evidence of technical rationality that ranks him between the Acheulian and Neanderthal men of the west, and nearer to the latter. Thus he is acquainted with pressure-flaking – pressing off, rather than striking, long narrow flakes inwards from the edge of such tools as hide scrapers. This is secondary flaking intended to complete the shape of a tool worked on a larger flake, which itself has been purposively struck from a larger core. Another piece has a carefully worked tang which makes it suitable as a javelin point.

From the lowest level in the Chou-k'ou-tien deposits where pieces of human workmanship were recovered (locality 13), through the most populous level (locality 1) to the upper level of habitation (locality 15), there is a gradual improvement of technique. The single piece from the earliest deposit does not yet show the skill described above, while those from locality 15 have points in common with the best Neanderthal work, the large flakes being struck from a core previously prepared to yield the desired shape in the detached fragment. Peking Man was gregarious, a hunter who returned to a permanent habitation. He split bones for their marrow, kept his dead near the hearth, and was probably a cannibal.

Although their habitat is less well established, there are a number of distinct types of man which are intermediate between Peking Man and modern man. The remains come from Kuantung, Hupei and Mongolia, dating to the middle and initial late Pleistocene, and belong to individuals more advanced in development than the more primitive representatives of the Neanderthal men of Europe and western Asia. Finally *Homo sapiens* emerges in the so-called Upper Cave Man discovered also at Chou-k'ou-tien, who is physically the equal of modern races. Judging from the skulls and other bones from the Upper Cave, and from some other roughly contemporary finds made in Szechwan and

Kwansi, the main features which distinguish the contemporary races of east Asia were already present in China during the deposition of the loess, i.e. the typical Chinese of the north and south, the Mongolian and the East Asian Tungusic types were already differentiated.

The date of Upper Cave Man should probably be put within 50,000 years of the present day. Between his time and the emergence of farming and the full neolithic way of life in the Yellow river valley, many other stone-using cultures of hunting and gathering communities appear in China. Unfortunately the topography was less favourable than that of western Europe for preserving their handiwork. Bone-carving and wall-painting do not survive as they do in France and northern Spain. But the general trend of technological evolution is similar in China to that in other parts of the world: as manual skill increased the flint and chert flakes were made smaller and narrower ('blades'), until the average knife had a cutting edge composed of several flakes mounted in a bone or wooden handle, and arrow points measured only a centimetre or two across.

This evolution occurred at the time when the yellow earth was still forming as a deposit of sand blown by powerful winds into north-west China from the colder regions of inner Asia. At the same time the plateau which is now Inner and Outer Mongolia was denuded of loose soil and lost its vegetation. On these bare uplands collections of the stone tools often lie on the surface, but without the traces of human activity which fill in the picture of Peking Man. It is certain that the bow was now the chief weapon, and well suited to hunting the rapid-moving game of the grassy uplands. The earliest evidence on the construction of the bow comes from Siberia, and belongs to the time when farming was beginning in China, although farther north the old palaeolithic life continued. The Siberian bow was built of several parts, of which the bone plaques lining the inner side survive in burials. This 'compound bow' was destined to be characteristic of China and the rest of East Asia until the introduction of firearms.

We have imagined the habitat of Lan-t'ien Man and his palaeolithic successors to be relatively open terrain of woods and grassland. After the deep loessic soil had formed in the northeast and central China (attaining depths of two and three hundred feet in places) the vegetation cover probably was still sparse, with no dense growth of forest. But we cannot conclude that the vast region lying either side of the *lower* reaches of the Yellow river was ecologically similar. Here the soil consists of a mixture of *re-deposited* loess and variously sorted gravels, loams and sands. From what we know of the recent history of the river we may conclude that even in early times it was inclined to raise its bed above the level of the surrounding fluviatile plain, and then, by breaking its banks, to flood widely and eventually even to change its principal course. (Just this happened in 1852, when the mouth changed from south of the Shantung peninsula to north of it.) The flood-plain was probably marshy, thickly covered in places with low and impenetrable vegetation.

With the discovery of farming and cattle-raising, which as in other parts of the world broadly coincided with the invention of pottery, weaving and the process of stone-polishing, new value was set on the possibility of settled life and the creation of larger social groups. On the loess, as the account given in the next section of this book shows, nature put few obstacles in the way of this revolutionary process. But east of the loessic zone settlement and communication must have been much more difficult, and probably man did not colonise the eastern flood-plain before the neolithic way of life was well established farther to the west. In the meantime to the south, in the basin of the Yangtze, palaeolithic methods persisted, with exclusive reliance on the hunt and fishing. Here the usual association of neolithic techniques is broken, for even after the making of pottery was learned, it is unlikely that the population turned immediately to settled farming.

2

View of the limestone hill where the remains of Lan-t'ien man were found in a deposit of reddish clay, 28 miles from Sian in Shensi. As in other parts of Asia and Europe, primitive man in China favoured a limestone environment which provided numerous shelters in caves and clefts.

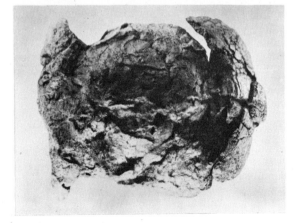

3

Top view of the skull-cap of Lan-t'ien man showing the extraordinary development of the supra-orbital ridge. The bone is clearly deformed by pressure from the deposits under which it was buried, and the surface partly eroded. Nevertheless a comparatively accurate reconstruction proved possible.

4

Lacking the superior flint used by primitive man elsewhere in Asia, the earliest inhabitants of China resorted to chert and quartz for their implements. These stones are more difficult than flint to shape by chipping. This quartz tool with a sharp lower edge served as a knife or scraper.

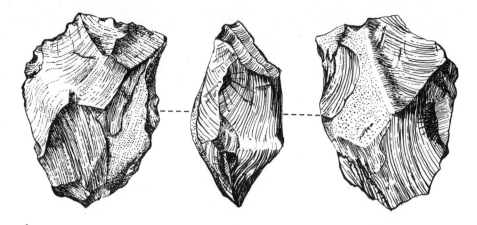

5
Three views of a chert tool (a knife or scraper) made by Peking Man. Part of the cortex remains, being left to give a good grip. The greater part of the edge was carefully sharpened by removing flakes from alternating positions along it. Such deliberately shaped pieces were, however, a small proportion of the total of stone broken by the inhabitants of the cave at Chou-k'ou-tien.

6
Two hand-axes shaped in chert from Ting-ts'un, Shansi. The larger is 18 cm long. It closely resembles a similar tool made by early Palaeolithic man in Europe, differing from European specimens mostly by reason of the coarser grain of the stone. The hand-axe was an all-purpose weapon and tool, being supplemented only by small scrapers, and spherical hammer stones.

7
Flint hand-axe of the Early Acheulian culture, found at the base of the middle gravels in the Thames valley. The superior control of a finer-grained material is to be contrasted with the working of the Ting-ts'un tools in fig. 6. The upper end, the grip, retains some of the original flint cortex. The broad flakes removed from the right edge have been struck off with wood.

8

Red pottery vase decorated with black painted design. The clay has been burnished before the pigment was applied; it was fired at a temperature above 1000° C. The rosettes of nine roundels are painted in white. Geometric ornament with reticulation and spirals was the chief resource of the neolithic potter in north-west China. The vase was shaped by hand. Found at Lan-chou. Height 18.3 cm. Late 3rd millennium BC.

2

Neolithic

The most complete remains of a food-producing, neolithic village ever excavated are to be seen preserved under a wide roof in Pan-p'o, an east suburb of Sian, in Shensi province. The seventy thousand square metres of the settlement are not exceptional for the neolithic communities which formed along the middle course of the Yellow river and along its western tributary, the Wei. In temperate Europe such a size is unheard of, for there the periodic exhaustion of the tilled land compelled even much smaller bands of farmers to move on. The Chinese villages were more permanent.

The first question that arises is how the fertility of the soil was maintained. The Yellow river did not flood periodically and deposit a fresh layer of soil over the plain, as did the Nile. Its flooding was, in any case, confined for the most part to the lower course of the river, east of the initial neolithic area. The answer seems to be in the nature of the *loess*, the yellow earth itself. Under the action of water, which the loess retains well, mineral salts are brought to the surface by capillary action, and so tend to re-fertilise the upper layer. It is clear that the neolithic farmers were aware of this special value of their land, for during the earlier part of the neolithic period their villages never spread beyond the margin of the yellow earth, and therefore kept fairly close to the great river and did not pass eastwards beyond the middle of Honan province.

On the basis of comparisons of Chinese painted neolithic pottery with similar potteries in south Russia and the Near East, it was once argued that the earliest neolithic culture had reached China by migration over a great distance. This has been finally refuted by the discovery, now backed by carbon-14 datings, that the pottery of central China is older than that to the north-west, which the supposed migration should have reached first. Nevertheless there is a puzzle in the suddenness of the adoption of farming in China, as the archaeological record now shows it. It is possible that the movements of the Yellow river across its bed even in the upper reaches has destroyed the trace of older and simpler neolithic communities, or buried them so deeply that they have escaped notice so far. The excavated village represents a culture which lasted approximately from 4500 to 3000 BC.

Some hundreds of villages resembling Pan-p'o, but the majority of them much smaller, were located on terraces along the river Wei, beginning with the second terrace above the present flood-plain. The terrain is not conducive to the formation of many small streams, and the supply of water for the irrigation which the long dry summers must have needed cannot have been easy. The loess banks tend to be high and vertical. Nevertheless, enough of the staple crop, millet, was produced to enable four or five hundred people to live in one place, and this would seem to require a system of irrigated fields. Irrigation demands

I

Bronze ting *for holding sacrificial meats. This type of vessel, with three legs or four, is one of the commonest of the ritual bronzes deposited in tombs of the Shang dynasty. T'ao-t'ieh monster masks are placed at the top of the legs. The bird motif enters Shang art towards the end of the dynasty. The geometrical ornament is purely decorative in intent. Height 21.7 cm. 12th–11th century BC.*

See pp. 37 ff.

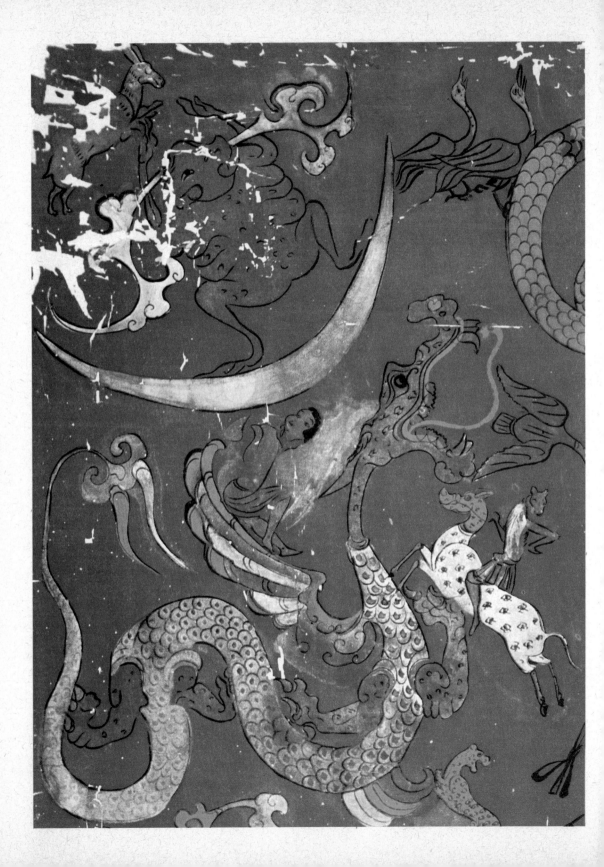

II

Detail of a painting on silk from Ma Wang Tui, the tomb of the Marquess of T'ai near Ch'ang-sha, Hunan. The frog and hare which inhabit the moon are seen at the top left, the lady Ch'ang-erh who also lives in a palace in the moon is shown riding through space on the wing of a dragon. Other parts of the painting show further spirits of the heavens and the underworld, a scene in the life of the Marquess, and the ceremony of her wake. Height of this detail approximately 22 cm. Early 1st century BC.
See pp. 55 ff.

a special degree of social cohesion and comparative security from warlike raids of neighbours.

Other signs of cooperative living noticed by the excavators add to the picture of a prosperous and well-organised tribal settlement. The whole village area is divided into three parts. One part is occupied by the houses, forty-six in number, and is surrounded by a ditch six metres deep, which was intended to collect the run-off during heavy rain rather than as a defensive feature, for it was not backed by a stockade. Beyond the ditch was set aside an area for burials and another for the pottery kilns. Among the houses is a larger, square one, whose ground plan implies a skilful timbering of the roof, and which was probably a village chief's dwelling, or, as the excavators prefer to interpret it, a communal meeting-place. Two oblong foundations of buildings which lack fireplaces and other tokens of human occupation are believed to be houses for the domesticated animals, which the abundant remains of bones show to have been principally pigs and dogs.

A curious feature of the houses is the lowering of the floors two or three feet below the ground level of the time. Considering the lingering of rain water on a dusty loess surface this arrangement had a distinct disadvantage, and it is not surprising to find that in every case the entrance of a house is divided from the interior by a low threshold surrounding the door and sometimes forming a short lobby with partition walls. On the other hand the lowered floor made it easier to frame the walls with timber and to build a conical roof which need not be over-large in order to give reasonable headroom. We may guess that timber of any length was already difficult to find in the central plain. It may only be a coincidence that these sunken floors are intermediate between the completely buried houses of the heavily wooded region north of the Amur, and the houses raised on stilts which are the earliest traced south of the Yangtze, and continue in use today in South-east Asia and the southern islands. Although the Pan-p'o houses had earth walls and roofs covered with a mixture of clay and straw, their bearing structure is entirely of wood. We see in them the beginning of the wooden pillar-and-beam architecture which continued throughout Chinese history until recent years. It is still practised in Korea and especially Japan, to which it was exported more than a thousand years ago.

Hunting with the bow and arrow was still an important, but not a crucial, supplement to the food supply at Pan-p'o, as is shown by some hundreds of bone arrowheads found scattered through the village. The chief quarry were species of deer, water-deer and sika, and the bamboo-rat (which is still eaten as a delicacy in parts of south-east Asia). But of equal if not greater importance was fishing, with which, on the evidence of designs painted on pottery, supernatural ideas were associated. A frequent motif of the potter-artist was a circular and diagrammatic human face, with ears which sometimes turn into fishes. Near to it is also a fish variously schematised. On other pots a large fish is painted alone, and the geometric transformation of its shape introduces us to a habit of Chinese art that was to have a very long history in the bronze age. Behind these drawings lies fisherman's magic, intended to increase the catch, the human face representing perhaps a god particularly concerned with this branch of fertility.

Around the houses were scores of deep storage-pits, in which grain was kept against the winter needs of the human and animal populations. Clothing was woven of coarse fibres and (judging from the large number of stone scrapers and pottery rubbers) included leather garments. The pottery, all hand-made and not turned, is likely to be women's work, though one supposes that the building and firing of the kilns would fall to the men. Temperatures around 1000° C could be reached, and pottery made of choice clay was baked to the greatest hardness which is possible in earthenware.

Apart from the decoration of the painted pottery there is little at Pan-p'o which suggests concern with unseen powers: there were no pottery idols or obvious talismans. In this respect the supernatural beliefs of the villagers seem to have resembled those of China in later ages, when no clear representations of gods were felt to be necessary, and religious iconography was mainly a matter of dragons and other monsters symbolising elemental forces.

Except for two cases of two and four persons buried together, the Pan-p'o burials are single. This practice rather tells against the theoretical claim made by the excavators that the neolithic society was matriarchal, for it is generally argued that *multiple* burials of families or septs of a clan related through the female line indicate a social organisation centred on women. The Pan-p'o graves are orientated with the head to the west or the north-west, and this custom is observed throughout the region of the Yangshao culture to which Pan-p'o belongs. A group of pots, fairly consistent in the choice of shape (a large jar, and one with round and one with pointed base), is placed with the corpse, which is regularly supine. Again we see a later custom anticipated: in the bronze age the grave gift of bronze vessels was also a fairly regular number of different vessels. In the graves which seem to belong to more important persons wooden coffins were used. Some simple stone beads and ornaments of cut shell appeared here and there, and the most elaborately decorated pieces are pottery bracelets. There were two examples of crescent-shaped stones which may have had particular meaning, for such things persist throughout the later neolithic period and survive into the bronze age to be made of jade. Eventually the written tradition informs us that these objects symbolise the heavens.

The neolithic age of East Asia is

divided into three broad cultural traditions corresponding to the valleys of the Amur, Yellow river and Yangtze. In the central zone which is thus defined, where the Yangshao (Pan-p'o) culture is equivalent to the earliest stage of settled farming, the Chinese tradition as we know it first took root. The middle stretch of the Yellow river, with the adjoining Wei tributary, is reasonably described as a nuclear area from which phases of change emanated in the later evolution and spread to other parts of China. In historical times the same area retained prime military and political significance.

The Yangshao culture was followed by the Lungshan neolithic, which ranged over the whole central plain in the third and early second millennium BC, although it never penetrated into the north-west. Superior Lungshan pottery is burnished-black, wheel-turned, and specialises in shapes which have a metallic look in their sharply angled profiles, although bronze-casting was not yet known. In Honan the succession of deposits exposed in excavations often shows Lungshan succeeding Yangshao and immediately preceding the Shang bronze age.

Around the relation of Yangshao and Lungshan turns an argument which has ideological overtones, for it involves views of the historical unity of Chinese culture, extending even as far back as the neolithic period. The official Chinese opinion is that the Lungshan culture is merely the later outcome of the Yangshao, having developed its characteristic traits in

precisely the same 'nuclear area'. In that case there would be no need to concede even an admixture of extraneous cultural elements in the genesis of Chinese civilisation, the culture of the men of Han. This theory not only presents an improbably narrow view of the formation of a national culture – all progress diffusing from Honan and Shensi – but builds on tenuous evidence of stratigraphy and typology.

The Lungshan culture develops its most characteristic forms, in settlement pattern, pottery and agriculture, in the eastern coastal zone, including that part of the Yellow river valley which consists of yellow earth mixed with loams and gravels as the result of river action. Some Lungshan traits connect with the far north-east and the Siberian neolithic, others with the south. In contrast with the Yangshao, millet, rice and possibly wheat were cultivated. Of necessity the settlements often sought out knolls above the flood-plain, and could not be so populous or enduring, and archaeologists have not reported any of the features symptomatic of the large cooperative community, such as were seen at Pan-p'o. People were buried with their heads to the east or the north-east, and flattish, rectangular stone axes with a neat perforation replace the pillow-shaped axes of Yangshao.

Nevertheless some features of Lungshan life – for instance, the custom of reading the future from heat-cracks in bone – were passed on to the Shang bronze-users, and a number of Lungshan pottery shapes provide the starting point for some highly individual types of Shang bronze vessels (the *ting* tripod and the *p'an* footed dish, for example). We are thus forced to the conclusion that the main development of Chinese material culture passed through an essential Lungshan stage, which incorporated into it characteristic features of the eastern neolithic tradition unknown in the 'nuclear area'.

In the northern zone of East Asia beyond the Amur river, and in the southern area comprising the Yangtze valley and the rolling country to the south of it, neolithic culture is less well understood. It was certainly impoverished and uninventive in comparison with its southern neighbours. The arts of pottery and stone-polishing do not combine here with agriculture and animal husbandry as they do in Yangshao and Lungshan. In Siberia the appearance of the bow and arrow is taken as the conventional criterion of neolithic culture, and in the Yangtze zone it is the production of rough varieties of pottery. In north and south hunting, fishing and gathering retained their basic importance until the eve of the bronze age and even afterwards. At a date archaeologists have not yet finally determined, rice cultivation was introduced in the south. As a sporadic crop, known to a few communities and a few favoured terrains, rice may be as ancient in this zone as millet farther north, but agricultural technique sufficient to establish settled communities of any size on the rice yield was probably not achieved until central China

was the scene of a flourishing bronze-using civilisation. Not long afterwards the southern territories were incorporated into the Chinese political state which had expanded from the middle Yellow river in all directions.

What, then, has become of Marxist theory in the Chinese interpretation of neolithic culture? Until the late 1930s Soviet archaeologists mostly expressed the view that all cultural evolution can be explained in strictly local terms, so that no external influence, or migration, may be invoked in accounting for change. After the Second World War the general philosophy of prehistory was modified. In any given cultural entity a need might arise, in the course of evolution, that is met by adopting a tool, or a social custom, or a technique such as agriculture, from another cultural sphere with which contact has been made. Before the need has arisen through its independent experience, no cultural group can learn by the example of its neighbours. Asian history abounds in examples of impassable cultural frontiers which are made intelligible in this way. Currently Chinese theorists accept a view of cultural diffusion, as distinct from local evolution, on the traditional European model, without formulating the nature of the resistance which such diffusion meets. They invoke the theory of unaffected independent evolution only for the nuclear area in Honan and Shensi, and derive from this region all the signs of economic and cultural advance which are observed elsewhere in the Chinese territories.

9 ABOVE
Excavation in progress at the neolithic village of Pan-p'o near Sian in Shensi. The rectangular depression is the floor of a house sunk below the ancient ground level. Various domestic fixtures were excavated in the loessic soil. Holes marking the position of timbers aided the reconstruction of the building on the lines shown in fig. 11.

10 BELOW
Drawings of a stylised human face and fish decorating a pottery bowl excavated at Pan-p'o. The ears of the face are shown as fish, resembling the fish drawn separately. Some examples show the latter stylised beyond recognition but the face is little altered. The insistence on fish may reflect a fisherman's magic intended to increase the catch.

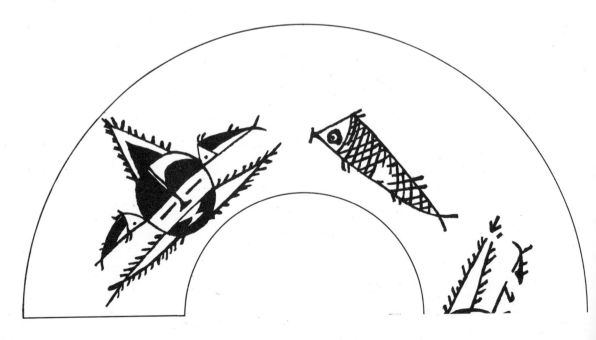

11 ABOVE

Reconstruction of a large square house at the neolithic village of Pan-p'o. The disposition of thicker and thinner pillars seems to indicate a sloping roof structure. Under the outer covering of the roof (reeds or millet stalks) was a layer of clay. The room measures about 11 by 13 metres.

12 BELOW

Reconstruction of a round house with sunken floor at Pan-p'o neolithic village. The lowering of the floor made roofing easier, but made the house liable to flooding by rainwater. The raised threshold was intended to keep the interior dry. The fireplace is here off centre since the middle of the floor was occupied by the main roof pillar.

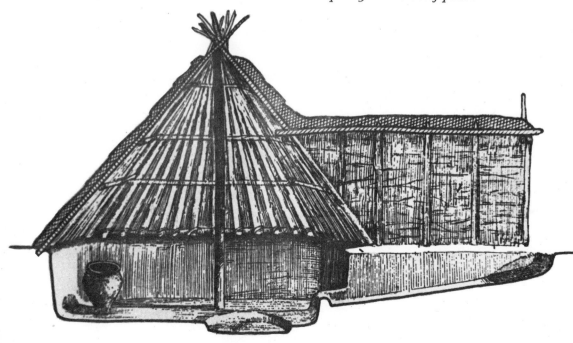

13

Pottery bowl with stars showing in white on a pink ground, found at P'ei-hsien, Kiangsu. Such painted pottery is rare in east China, falling in the middle stage of the Neolithic. Height 18.5 cm. Late 4th or 3rd millennium BC.

14

Fragments of pot rims from Pan-p'o neolithic village, with symbols scratched through the paint to the clay beneath, referring perhaps to owners, or makers. They cannot be closely connected with Chinese writing as established later, but the idea of the ideograph may be present. 3rd or early 2nd millennium BC.

15 FACING

Pottery jug of the type called k'uei, made of whitish clay, from Wei-fang, Shantung. This type is confined to the east coast, its sculptural quality anticipating the design of the later bronze sacrificial vessels. Height 29.7 cm. 3rd or early 2nd millennium BC.

16

Bronze ceremonial axe, yueh, *as found placed in Shang graves at the edge of the burial chamber. The mask suggests human physiognomy, but in general is assimilated to the* t'ao-t'ieh *monster. Such axes were used in beheading the human victims placed in royal tombs, and in sacrificial pits connected with religious or ceremonial buildings. Height 25 cm. British Museum. 14th–12th century BC.*

3

The Bronze Age

The Chinese bronze age differs from the equivalent periods of history in the Near East and Europe in one remarkable way. It seems to spring from the ground fully-fledged technologically: its earliest bronze-casting demonstrates a skill and sophistication which in Europe equates with the culture of La Tène in the first millennium BC, and in the Near East would be matched to some extent, but not surpassed, by work of the mid-second millennium BC. It is just at this time, about 1700–1500 BC, that the beginning of bronze metallurgy in China is dated. Before then, however, there was not, as one finds in Europe and the Near East, a long period of rudimentary bronze-working, in which technique is gradually improved to the advanced standard attained by the time iron begins to displace bronze as the leading metal.

The date of the latter event is approximately the same in the West and in China, the fifth and fourth century BC, although in China iron was slower in displacing bronze. The tardiness of the general adoption of iron also distinguishes the Chinese Bronze Age from the economic evolution of the West. The explanation lies partly in the monopolistic tendencies of rulers in the city states into which China was soon split – the control of bronze was one source of their power – and partly in the near-starvation livelihood of a vast inert peasantry whose purchasing power for metal, or any manufactured goods, was minimal.

In a shadowy way the Chinese have always known the site of the last Shang capital, which in literature is called Yin-hsü, 'The Waste of Yin', Yin being an alternative name for the dynasty. But the exact location was forgotten, and to the literary-minded antiquarians in the long-standing Chinese tradition exactness in such things did not matter: only *inscriptions* could not be ignored. In the last two years of the nineteenth century thousands of fragments of inscribed tortoise-shell and bone came to light outside the modern village of Hsiao-t'un, near Anyang in north Honan. At first they passed only into the hands of apothecaries as 'dragon bones', to be ground as medicine. Then Wang I-jung, a member of the Imperial Academy resident in Peking, recognised the inscriptions for what they were: the earliest-known form of Chinese writing. Wang committed a patriot's suicide in 1900 when foreign troops occupied the capital, but the news spread, and the learned began to collect the bones for scholarship and the unlearned for the profit they could make by their sale.

At Hsiao-t'un marvellous bronze vessels were also dug up, mostly by local villagers who had devised a means of using a long probe to locate them. These came through dealers into collections in China and abroad, but it was not until 1915 that Lo Chen-yü traced the bones to their true source, and realisation dawned upon the learned world that this place could be

III

A decorative bronze plaque depicting a wild boar attacked by two hunting cheetahs. A snake is biting the tail of the upper assailant. The back of the bronze is plain, suggesting that it was mounted on a flat surface. Such realistic art is characteristic of the barbarian kingdom of Tien in ancient Yünnan. Length 17.1 cm. 2nd or early 1st century BC.
See pp. 55 ff.

IV

White porcellaneous bowl covered with clear glaze.
The ornament imitates the jewels and medallions of
Iranian art, while the petals of the base derive from
the lotus frequent in Buddhist art. Such pieces mark
the beginning of a long-lived tradition of white
porcelain manufactured in north China. Found at
Han-sen-chai, near Sian, Shensi. Height 23 cm.
From a tomb dated to AD 667.
See pp. 77 ff.

no other than the Waste of Yin, or, as the inscriptions themselves called it, the city of Great Shang. Scientific investigation of the site was not undertaken until 1928. By this time much was known of Shang culture from the study of the inscribed bones and the bronze vessels.

The Shang dynasty begins a cycle of bronze-age civilisation which evolved without interruption or revolutionary change from about the sixteenth until the third century BC. For some three centuries at least Shang kings ruled central China from Cheng-chou in Honan, then moved north to the vicinity of Anyang. Their domain comprised the eastern part of what had been the realm of the Yangshao neolithic. The end of the dynasty came in 1027 BC when it was overthrown in an invasion from northwestern China headed by the house of Chou. Thereafter, although the details of political history are immensely complicated and increasingly well recounted in history, the broad pattern of events was monotonously simple. The Chou divided the country into principalities, which extended to the east coast and the Yangtze. Many of these 'feudal' states were very small. The greater ones soon forgot their theoretical allegiance to the Chou king and began to war among themselves. The variety of alliances and patterns of warfare and territorial exchange which constitute Chinese history until the unification of 221 BC indicates no great change in the social order or the economic basis of life. Improved agriculture led to an explosive increase in population, and periodically more

lethal weapons were introduced into the endless internecine carnage against which philosophers, Confucius among the first, protested in vain.

Among weapons first came the bronze halberd, the bronze-tipped arrow and the fighting chariot, the mainstay of the Shang army. Much later, about 500 BC, a short bronze sword was adopted, and soon afterwards the cross-bow and the long iron sword were decisive in the fortunes of war. The warriors of the western highland zone were ultimately the supreme victors, and in 221 BC Shih Huang Ti of Ch'in became the first emperor of the whole of China as we know it today. By this date China had entered the iron age, but the Ch'in victory is seen as closing a phase of bronze-age society and initiating a new centralisation and a new social order. Chinese theorists interpret the Shang age, and its sequel down to 475 BC, as the 'slave-owners' state', which is followed by a 'feudalism' lasting until the revolution of 1912.

The picture we have today of Shang civilisation owes more to archaeological work than to the accounts, so incomplete and moralised, which survive in written history. The most characteristic and informative excavations are of 'royal' tombs and of chariot burials. One of the former was investigated at Yi-tu in Shantung province in 1965. A central rectangular shaft, 8.25 metres deep and 15 by 10.5 metres at the surface, descends with slightly inward-sloping walls to a step near the base, below which the wooden funeral chamber had been built over a protective layer of charcoal.

The timbers framing the chamber had decayed leaving no trace, but some of the typical features of a great Shang tomb were preserved. Below the funeral chamber were three other pits, the deepest containing the skeleton of a human funeral victim, buried in a seated position and wearing a bone pin in his (or her – the sex was not established) hair. This was the basal sacrifice, a first propitiation of the spirits of the underworld. There followed, in smaller pits a little higher, the body of a dog, buried with some meat for his food, and the supine body of a human victim lacking this thoughtful provision. In the latter case also we can assume that he was buried alive: the legs are broken and a wooden post of which traces were found is interpreted as serving to tie the man down.

Further human victims, this time in wooden coffins and so perhaps of superior status, were buried on the step above the funeral chamber. From the latter, cuttings led to the surface towards the four cardinal directions though, according to the rule, only the southern approach went quite to the bottom of the shaft, providing the main entry. Where this debouched into the space of the funeral chamber twenty-four human skulls and thirteen human skeletons, all of young men, were buried in three layers, having evidently been slaughtered *in situ* to mark the occasion.

Of the principal occupant of this tomb no trace was found. The funeral chamber had been robbed at least three times in antiquity, but there still remained fragments of ritual bronze vessels, spearheads, arrowheads, symbolic jade objects (the crescent representing the heavens and a halberd blade), cowrie-shell money, and, at the edge of the step around the funeral chamber, two massive bronze axeheads. These last were symbols of office – the sign of the axe is well known in Shang inscriptions – and perhaps simultaneously the emblem of a powerful clan. The scale and sumptuous furnishings of the tomb, with so many people sent to accompany their dead master, must indicate royalty, or membership of a small ruling group. In Anyang, the capital of the second half of the dynasty, great shaft graves with cruciform approaches from the surface are certainly the tombs of kings, their rich contents of bronze, jade and slaughtered victims exceeding even what was found at Yi-tu.

The shafts of all these tombs are filled with thin layers of hard-rammed earth. (At Yi-tu layers of sandy and loamy soil alternated for greater cohesion.) The same method was followed in building walls (for example, the temple and palace complex in Sector C at Anyang). It is curious that sun-dried brick was never resorted to, in the Near Eastern fashion. With fuel, particularly the heavier kind of timber, in comparatively short supply in the Chinese central plain, it is less surprising that burnt brick was not employed.

The Shang oligarchs were literate, or their scribes and diviners were, using ideograms which began as abbreviated pictures and were developed by indicator and punning phonetic much in the manner of Egyptian and Sumerian writing. Already the language seems to have had many words spoken alike, as the modern language descended from it has to a still greater degree. Today, for example, the three words pronounced *zhu*, meaning to *reside, a post, to pour*, are differentiated by combining with the same ideogram the additional indicators 'man', 'tree', 'water'. The phonetic part of these words, a symbol always read *zhu* or something approximating to that, when it stands alone means 'master'.

Shang kings consulted the spirits of their ancestors, and other divinities such as Ruler of the Four Quarters, Western Mother, and Shang Ti the supreme god, offering animal and human sacrifice to them and putting questions on the acceptability of the sacrifices and some more practical matters. The question was written on tortoise-shell, or more often on animal shoulder bones (these are the supposed dragon bones!), and answer sought by cracking the bone with fire. The oracle indicated its wishes or advice by determining the shape of the cracks, though how these were read by the diviner is not now known. The names of kings recorded in the oracle sentences confirm the list transmitted to history, and the mention of frontier enemies, crops, royal journeys, all help to fill in a picture of the Shang state. It is not an unfamiliar one to anyone acquainted with the ancient history of Mesopotamia. Ur of the Chaldees was a city-state ruled under a kind of theocracy comparable to that of Shang, no less interested in divination, a small class of city-based warriors lording it over submissive land-tied peasants.

In west and east the chariot was the supreme bronze-age arm, swiftly giving tactical advantage. It also conferred status as the typical contribution of the wealthy subjects to the bulwarks of the state. The design of the Chinese chariot is surprisingly close to that of chariots known in western Asia and the Caucasus about the middle of the second millennium BC, so the suggestion is close at hand that somehow the invention was communicated to the valley of the Yellow river. While no contacts can be demonstrated that account for this, absolute independence of the two vehicles is difficult to accept. But the Chinese chariot has some distinctive features, the most striking being the skilful structure of the wheels. Thanks to the nature of the loessic soil, archaeologists have recovered some exact models of both the Shang and later chariots.

Model is the correct term here. The process which preserved the shape is that which was first exploited by the excavators of the Sutton Hoo ship in East Anglia. Surrounded by an even-textured soil (in China the loess), the wooden parts of buried objects were replaced, as they decayed away, by finer particles of the soil, which subsequently hardened more than the surrounding filling of the burial, or at least retained a distinct appearance. Thus the excavators needed only to remove the unwanted filling to reveal the shape of the wooden structure by a ghost answering to its every detail. Burial of chariots complete with their two horses and the driver – sometimes with a second man – was an established custom under the Shang, and more than half a dozen well-preserved examples have been excavated at the Anyang capital. Some of these were in the temple area, part of a considerable spread of buried military victims, amounting it would seem to an army unit.

The latest chariot excavation took place in 1972, also at Anyang, just south of the village called Hsiao-min-t'un. The stout shaft of the vehicle is half-joined to the centre of an axle of similar weight, and over this crossing the fenced driver's platform was laid on a rectangular frame. Harnessing was by means of yokes resting on the horses' necks and bands passing around the necks, so that the lines represented by rows of decorative bronze rondels in the grave are likely to mark reins rather than traces. The bronze parts include axle-caps, mounts on the yokes, an ornament for the rear end of the shaft protruding just beyond the box; but no trace was found of nails or crampons, and it is to be concluded that the main members of the structure were held together by keying and lashing with perishable materials. In this grave the charioteer was buried stretched just behind his box, and supine, whereas a prone position of the corpse was usual in formal Shang burials of every class (a custom surviving in central China from the neolithic period). Both driver and horses had been covered with mats of some kind. Evidently they had all been laid in position before the chariot itself was lowered into the pit.

The custom of burying chariots persisted for some five or six centuries after the end of the Shang dynasty. Oracle-taking by fire and the whole-sale slaughter of human victims had ceased. In great tombs, however, a few retainers might be placed to accompany their master to the Yellow Springs, and until Han times bronze vessels continued to be the chief grave gifts. Variously apportioned to meat and grain offerings, and the wine libation, these vessels are the main source of our knowledge of Chinese art in the pre-Han period. They remain one of the wonders of the world for the splendour of their ornament and their technical accomplishment. The Shang method of casting in piece-moulds continued for some five hundred years afterwards. Then one-piece moulds made by encasing a wax model were adopted, a technique universal in the ancient Near East and Europe, but mysteriously lacking in the earlier phase of the Chinese Bronze Age.

The warfare of the last few centuries of the Chou era, the Period of the Warring States, at last resolved itself into the struggle of two great kingdoms: Ch'in, whose power was based on the western highlands; and Ch'u, which had long controlled the middle Yangtze and much to the north and south of it. In 221 BC Ch'in was finally victorious, and the whole of China was united under a single ruler for the first time. The Great Wall was completed on the northern frontier, and a civil service was organised to administer a despotic and efficient government. When the founder of the Han dynasty dismissed the second Ch'in emperor in 206 BC, he at once set about organising a bureaucratic state on foundations provided by his predecessors.

17

Bronze vessel, ting, for holding sacrificial meats, excavated at Ning-hsiang, Hunan. This is the only piece of its kind decorated with human faces, which may allude to victims of the rite. On the inside are cast the ideographs for ta ho. This means 'large grain', or 'great crop', but it may also denote the name of a person or clan. The ting was found south of the Yangtze, and marks the southern limit of the territory in which Shang rule and culture extended. Height 38.7 cm. 14th–12th century BC.

18 FACING

Tripod bronze vessel, chia, intended for wine used in religious libation. On it the design of the t'ao-t'ieh monster is dissolved into scrolling, leaving only the eyes immediately visible. The function of the capped pillars rising from the lip is unknown, possibly they served to raise the chia by means of tongs when the wine it held was heated. Excavated at Fei-hsi, Anhui. Height 53.5 cm. 13th–11th century BC.

20 BELOW
The Przewalsky horse, an Asian steppe breed similar to the horses which drew Shang chariots. This animal belonged to a herd on the estate of the Duke of Bedford.

Earth-cast of a chariot recently excavated at Hsiao-min-t'un, near Anyang, Honan. Some bronze harness parts and ornaments remain over the horses' skeletons. The yokes which rested on the horses' necks when they were harnessed appear at the forward end of the shaft, capped by bottle-shaped bronze ornaments. The structure of the charioteer's box, the large hubs and fine spokes are typical of Shang chariots; the charioteer was killed at the funeral and his body placed just behind his vehicle. 13th–11th century BC.

A set of ox scapulae laid in order as a buried archive, after their use in oracle taking. The marks visible on the surface are (a) incisions made with a chisel, (b) alongside each incision a burnt patch where the bone was touched with a red-hot bronze point. On some of the scapulae the question put to the oracle was inscribed alongside the incisions. The majority of these concern the conduct of sacrificial rite, but others demand answers to more mundane questions. The answers were read, by a method unknown today, from cracks produced by the heat on the other side of the shoulder bone. 12th–11th century BC.

Jade ornaments of the Shang and early Chou dynasties. All are worked on thin plaques of jade. The white bird on the right appears frequently in Shang art as an emblem of some kind, possibly denoting an animistic deity, protector of the royal house. The smaller bird on the left, a stylised swallow, is another frequent design in Shang. The remaining pieces belong to the 10th–8th centuries BC. The cormorant with a fish is known only in jade. The dragon with its tail ending in another head is the point of departure for a new formulation of the animal ornament. Length of the large bird 13 cm. 12th–8th century BC. British Museum.

23

Ceremonial halberd consisting of an engraved jade blade set in a bronze haft. The latter is decorated with designs of dragons and formal motifs of the kind found also cast on the ritual vessels. The work is inlaid with malachite. Length 34.3 cm. 13th–11th century BC. Freer Gallery of Art, Washington.

24

Musical stone from the royal tomb at Wu-kuan-ts'un, Anyang, Honan. The stone was intended to be suspended by a cord and struck. (By about 500 BC complete chimes of such stones were in use, sounding a scale of nine or thirteen notes rising in tones and semitones and combining in fourths and fifths.) Length 81 cm. 12th–11th century BC.

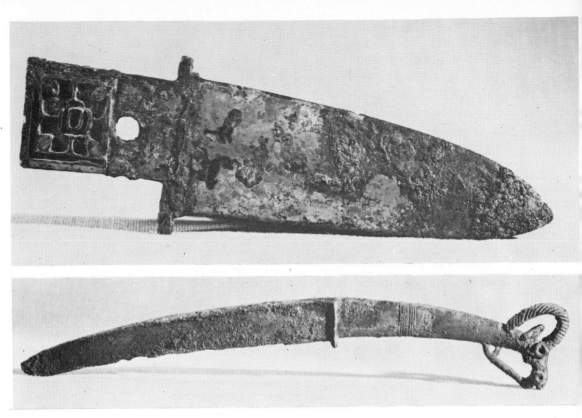

25

Bronze halberd blade and knife, the armament of Shang warriors. The halberd on a haft three or four feet long was the regular weapon of infantry. The charioteer, whose chief arm was the bow, carried also a knife, whose decoration (here an ibex head) falls outside the usual range of Shang art. Lengths about 20 and 22 cm. 12th–11th century BC. British Museum.

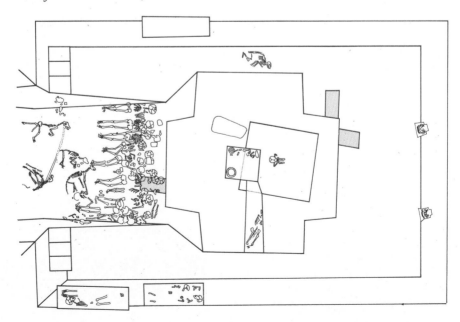

27

Bronze vessel, kuang, *for mixing wine, cast in the 10th century BC, at the beginning of the Chou dynasty. The jawless* t'ao-t'ieh *mask, and the dragons related to it, provide most of the ornament. Stylised birds fill the lower zone. The friendly monster into which the lid of the vessel is shaped begins as a bull with snail-like horns, and ends with a peacock's tail. Height 31.6 cm. Excavated at Fu-feng, Shensi. 10th century BC.*

26 FACING

Plan of the Shang tomb at Yi-tu. Beheaded victims line the approach to the burial chamber. The latter was constructed of timbers over a basal sacrificial pit in which a dog was placed. The axes placed at one edge of the tomb shaft were probably used in the course of the bloody funeral. 13th–11th century BC.

28

Bronze wine pourer, ho, combining in its ornament ancient motifs with some new ideas. The design on the side derives from a dragon motif. The newer elements are the bird lid and the shape of spout and handle. The whole is alien to the official art of Shang and of the early Chou period, and heralds a transformation of the animal style. Height 38 cm. Excavated at Fu-feng, Shensi. 9th century BC.

29 RIGHT

Bronze mask and ring from the wooden door of a burial chamber built at the bottom of a shaft. In this case the casting was preceded by an exact wax model, in contrast to earlier methods using piece moulds. The mask revives the idea of the t'ao-t'ieh, composing it of entirely new elements: serpentine dragons, a plumed bird of prey and new geometric detail. The dragons of the ring are represented as encircling it. Excavated at Yi-hsien, Hopei. Length of the mask 45 cm. 5th century BC.

Fragment of lacquer-painted wood depicting a tamer of dragons. Subjects of this kind, first appearing in Chinese art in the 4th century BC, relate to a mythology more fully represented in the Han period, which was part of a body of Taoist lore. The dragon-tamer has wings below his arms and the emblem of an immortal on his head. This iconography breaks completely with that of the Shang-Chou tradition of hieratic art, as seen in the sacrificial bronzes. Excavated at Hsin-yang, Honan. 4th century BC.

31

In 221 BC the first emperor of the house of Ch'in conquered the whole of China and united it under his rule. One of his first tasks was to extend and complete the walls erected to protect the northern Chinese states against the inroads of nomadic invaders. With later repair and elaboration, this is the Great Wall of China, here seen at its eastern end north of Peking. Camels had their use along the northern routes until recent times. (Photo A. Brankston.)

32 FACING

The tomb of the first Ch'in emperor, Shih Huang Ti, is the most impressive surviving in China. It was plundered shortly after the funeral but has not been excavated since. The main mound and burial chamber were anciently reported to contain vast and amazing treasure. On the periphery of the precinct, about half a kilometre from the mound, there appear to have been offering chapels furnished with such pottery figures of servitors as this one. The realism and dignity of the pose mark a new departure in Chinese sculpture. Height 64.5 cm. Late 3rd century BC.

33

Bronze figure of a horse flying past a swallow. The Chinese military intervention in central Asia at the end of the 2nd century BC made contact with the Persian empire, and among other things obtained a breeding stud of the tall and fast horses native to Sogdiana and Ferghana. These were celebrated by poet and artist—as, in contrast to the earlier stumpy horse known to the Chinese, it well deserved to be (see fig. 20). This outstanding example of a new realistic sculpture comes from the tomb of a general excavated at Wu-wei, Shensi. Height 34.5 cm. 2nd century AD.

4

The Han Empire

The Han empire can be compared in many ways with its part-contemporary, the Roman empire. Autocratic emperors ruled from capitals at Sian in Shensi and Loyang in Honan, conducted campaigns of 'pacification' in the outlying regions of China proper, and sent expeditions against neighbouring peoples as far as the borders of Persia in the west and the Korean peninsula in the east. Southwards Han power extended into the territory of Annam, the modern North Vietnam. Well-constructed roads were built to meet military needs. The organisation of frontier troops, with veterans' colonies and efficient systems of signalling and reporting, recall the Roman model, and methods of taxation were as productive and as uniformly applied as in the West. On the other hand, the Chinese efforts to repress the growth of merchant wealth, in keeping with the dictates of political theory, contrast with the encouragement which the Roman legal system gave to the development of trade. Chinese emperors did not experience even the vestigial restraints on personal rule which survived in the Roman empire from the days of the Republic.

Archaeology throws light on three aspects of the culture of the Han period. In the earlier half of the dynasty, the Western Han, an aristocratic tradition survives in the ruling class and prolongs the art of pre-Han time. Then in the first century AD comes a dramatic change, with the rise of realism in pictorial art, which now portrays much of ordinary life, rejecting the impersonal conventions of the predominantly decorative art of the past. Thirdly, the art and diverse ideology of barbarian neighbours, who were in the course of assimilation and annexation by the Chinese, can be contrasted with the metropolitan culture. This aspect is ideally shown in bronzes excavated in the south-western province of Yünnan, belonging to the kingdom of Tien.

The most informative of recent discoveries shows us the domestic appurtenances of an imperial prince. In 1968 an engineering platoon of the People's Liberation Army was digging a tunnel in a low hill near Manch'eng in Hopei, near Peking, when a five-metre-deep hollow was found below, leading to a large and straight man-made passage. The report runs: 'Flashlight in one hand and gun in the other the fighters jumped into the hollow and moved along the tunnel. It was cold and dry. As they went along they saw broken tiles on the ground, and skeletons of horses and remains of chariots by the side.' The carriages proved to be six in number. The soldiers reconnoitred this tunnel, coming to a place where two branches led to either side at right angles, their farther ends lost in the darkness. In front was a large chamber, ten by thirteen metres, and six metres high, on the floor of which were spread in order scores of bronze and pottery vessels, stone figurines and parts of chariots. In the far wall of this 'middle chamber' (as it proved to be) was a door consisting of two massive stone slabs. These were negotiated by climbing through a free space above them, and opened from the inside. The inner chamber was found to be built also of stone slabs, with a slanting roof, part of which had collapsed. The floor was covered with similar slabs, on which lay dead vegetation apparently fallen from the roof. When this rubbish was cleared away a white marble platform was revealed, whereon lay fragments of wood and lacquer paint which were all that remained of a sumptuous coffin. Under and among this debris was a suit consisting entirely of jade tablets, made to encase a man from head to toe, not omitting a handsome codpiece.

Inscriptions on some of the bronze vessels identified this tomb as that of Liu Sheng, an elder brother of the emperor Wu Ti, who bore the title of King Ching, holding land in fief at Ching-shan (which is the district of Hopei in which the tomb is situated), and had died in 113 BC. The historian attributes no important role to him, but comments that he was fond of wine and women. The many wine vessels among his grave gifts were not inappropriate. The entrance to the tomb was located on the hillside near to a heap of broken rock which evidently was the spoil from the tunnel digging. One hundred metres to the north a similar heap was noticed, and this proved to be the entrance to another similar tomb, in which, also

wearing a jade suit, the lady Tou Wan, wife of Liu Sheng, was buried. She had followed her husband into the mountainside about ten years after his death.

It had not previously been realised that the 'jade cases' and 'jade garments' of historical texts were perhaps closely fitting suits like those found at Manch'eng. Applied to garments, 'jade' might have indicated ornaments added to them, or referred to their magnificence in general. But funeral superstition about jade was very ancient in China, beginning in the neolithic period with the placing of symbolic jade rings in graves. At the beginning of the Han period, with the resurgence, particularly among the members of the official and ruling classes, of the magical beliefs that form part of the Taoist tradition, the practice arose of providing a buried corpse with nine jade objects designed to stop the nine orifices of the human body, a cicada being intended to lay on the tongue. The theory put forward by Taoist pundits, however, was that jade prevented the putrefaction of the corpse. Just what advantage was thought to accrue thereby to the deceased is not made clear in any surviving Chinese literature, which is uniformly reticent on the subject of the afterworld. The articulate and literate classes at least professed reverence and love towards the dead, observing the pieties of commemoration and simple offerings of incense and food. They mostly ignored Taoist tales of underworld spirits waiting to be placated. Even after the arrival of Buddhism, with its talk of paradise, hell and judges of the dead, they did not care to formulate precise beliefs about what awaited them on the other side.

Liu Sheng and his wife went to extremes in having their whole bodies encased in jade. Such ostentation was perhaps not uncommon among the Han gentry, though it had not been previously verified archaeologically. His suit divides into thirteen parts and hers into twelve, being composed of 2690 and 2160 tablets respectively. The tablets are mostly rectangular and measure a few centimetres across, attached by gold wire passed through perforations at the corners. His gold wire amounts to 1100 grammes, but hers only to 700 grammes, for the tablets of the female bodice were held in place by silk piping gummed to a backing of heavy cloth. When they were found, the jade suits had collapsed, the corpses perished to a few traces. Reconstituted on aluminium frames, the suits are now the most impressive exhibits of the Peking Historical Museum.

In each case the middle chambers of the tombs had contained a now vanished wooden building roofed by tiles, from which seepage was drained away by a rather elaborate system of channels and holes cut in the rock floor. Both tombs were closed in the same way: between two walls of rammed earth or brick molten iron was poured to form an impenetrable metal curtain barring the entrance. It is thanks to this most effective sealing that the contents remained inviolate. The most prominent among them are gilded and inlaid bronzes, such as the cloud scroll *hu* (fig. 36) and the four leopards which served to weigh down the corners of a silk pall long ago fallen to dust. Some of the ornamental parts of these objects reveal an interest in Taoist theories of the cosmic structure, which were now attracting the attention of the educated class. Below the cosmic mountain which forms the apex of a 'vast mountain censer' the White Tiger, spirit of the west, bites the tail of the Red Bird, spirit of the south.

It was the emperor Wu Ti (140–85 BC) who most actively pursued the policy of territorial expansion. Towards the end of the second century BC he was engaged in putting down a rebellion of tribes on the south coast of China. In 109 BC, when this was completed, he turned his attention to the Tien people of Yünnan, who lived around the lake of that name near the modern city of Kunming. The Tienians were suspected of having given assistance to the recent rebels, and deserved to be chastised. But their king made his submission to the emperor before the expedition against them set off. Until a few years ago nothing was known of the culture of the Yünnan barbarians beyond the brief record given by the historian Ssu-ma Ch'ien, who wrote shortly after their capitulation. He describes them as seminomadic raisers of cattle, divided into many tribes, whose king claimed descent from the ancient Chinese kings of the southern Ch'u state, and whose culture was consequently based upon that of China herself.

In 1946 Dr N. D. Fraser of the Scottish Mission to Lepers was in Kunming and in a shop noticed some interesting ancient bronze being broken for melting down. The pieces which he acquired and afterwards presented to the British Museum revealed a decorative art and bronze technique distinct from those of Han. In 1952 when Chinese archaeologists conducted extensive excavations on the hill of Shih-chai-shan, site of the necropolis of Tien kings from which Dr Fraser's bronzes possibly came, a wealth of material was revealed, and a culture of immense significance for the early history of the whole of southeast Asia was put on the map.

Most intriguing are large bronze drums, originally intended to stand with the striking surface upwards, which had been converted into containers by sealing the bottom. These were found full of cowrie shells, a form of currency which had circulated in China itself a thousand years earlier. On the top surface of the drums was, in most cases, attached a circular bronze plate on which the scene of a battle or a village festival or ceremony is represented by small separate figures cast in bronze. The motive behind the compositions – careful portrayal of scenes of real life – is one rare in metropolitan China before the first century

BC (i.e. a century later than the Shih-chai-shan bronzes). The skill of the Tien artist lay in relating his people together dramatically and in natural poses. His genius for realism goes even farther in representing animals, which were multiplied in bronze for their own sake, or placed – awkwardly enough from a practical point of view – on axes and daggers. In animal combats leopards attack a more docile or domestic species. The theme is one well known in the art of the nomads inhabiting the steppes thousands of miles to the north, but no direct connection between the two cultures can yet be established.

Enough material originating from central China was present in the Tien tombs to show that trade or the exchange of gifts with the Chinese was frequent. In contrast to this, the native Tienian products point culturally in two opposite directions. The weapons, battle axes and halberds, resemble types which were in use in China some eight hundred years earlier, although it is not clear where the tradition can have been preserved in the interim. The drums, on the other hand, stand at the fountain-head of a tradition of art and ceremony which became widespread throughout south China, Thailand, Malaya and the islands of the south seas generally. The Karen people of Burma were found to be manufacturing these drums when Europeans first made their acquaintance late in the nineteenth century. In most parts of South-east Asia the drums are preserved in Buddhist temples or the sacred houses of villages, and are explained as precious heirlooms, to be sounded on special occasions. There is mention of their use in a rain-making ceremony, although this application need not have been universal (indeed in the region there is not much need to invoke rain ceremonially). A study of the evolving shapes of the drums and their ornament points strongly to Yünnan as the centre from which their manufacture spread, and thus supports the theory that the bronze age of south-east Asia was much influenced from south-west China. The figural art of Tien, however, was not exportable, and is unmatched elsewhere.

The grounds on which the Tienians claimed connection with the Chinese are curious. It is said that Chuang Ch'iao, the royal Ch'u relative, invaded Tien in the 330s BC, but found his retreat cut off – by a move of the Ch'in army which took place at least fifty years later! So Chuang Ch'iao settled in Tien as its king, his men took local wives and founded a Chinese state with Chinese culture. Although Chinese writers still do not question this account, there can be little doubt that it is a dynastic fiction aimed at dignifying the Tien line of kings by connecting it with Chinese princes, especially as Chuang Ch'iao figures elsewhere in Chinese literature as an obviously legendary bandit and trouble-maker. By the middle of the first century BC the usefulness of Tien, whose king held the gold seal and purple ribbon issued to the head of a client state, had ceased, and the bar-

barian kingdom disappears from history, absorbed into the Han territorial system.

Wu Ti's more important foreign adventure, into Central Asia, also leaves its trace in artefacts committed to the tombs of great officers. In 128 BC Wu Ti's emissary Chang Ch'ien, after an interrupted journey of ten years, reached Sogdiana, the eastern province of the Persian empire, lying between the Oxus and the Jaxartes. He had travelled nearly three thousand miles along the route that was later to become the Silk Road. On his return to Sian, the Han capital, he reported that a remarkable type of horse was bred in Sogdiana. The emperor at once determined to obtain some of these animals as an invaluable mount for his armies facing hordes of nomad riders on the north-western frontier. But it was not until the turn of the century, after dispatching an army of 60,000 to defeat the Sogdians before their own capital, that his aim was achieved. The contrast of the new 'celestial', 'blood-sweating' horse from the west with the breed on which the Chinese had previously relied is seen by comparing statues of 118 BC from the tomb of a frontier commander with figurines recently discovered in Shensi which date to the first century BC and the first century AD. The new horses are tall, sinewy and nervous, the old type low and stolid. Artistic skill was lavished on the models of the superior animals, and they appear in the processions of carriages which are often painted on the walls of tombs.

V

Pottery figurine of a mounted huntsman in trouble with a hunting cheetah riding on the crupper of his horse. The beard and pointed cap show the man to be a Central Asian. This excellent example of the realistic art of T'ang came from the tomb of the Princess Yung Tai. Height 31.5 cm. AD 706.
See pp. 77 ff.

VI, VII

Paintings on the walls of Princess Yung Tai's tomb.
The officials standing beside horses and a rack with
pikes appear on the side of the long approach corridor
sloping down to the burial chamber. In the ante-room
of the burial chamber are paintings of the women
who attended the Princess, of which a detail is
shown here. AD 706.

See pp. 77 ff.

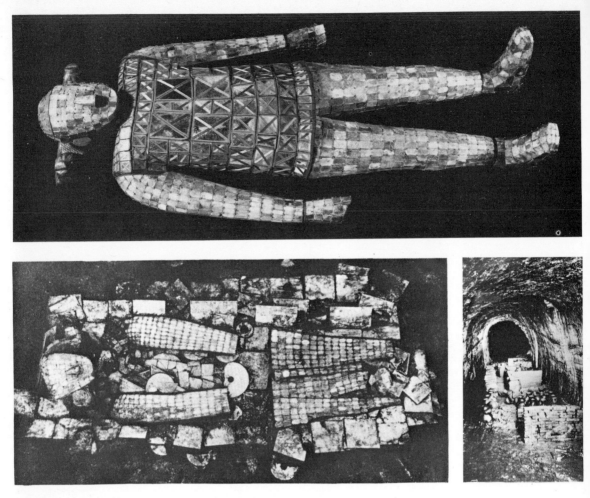

34

The jade funeral suit of Liu Sheng's wife, the Princess Tou Wan, as found (below) in her rock-hewn tomb alongside her husband's, and restored (above). The suit consists of over 2000 tablets tied together with knotted gold wire, or, in the case of the bodice, attached by silk piping gummed to a cloth lining. The head rests on a pillow ending on either side in animal heads. The jade, originally light green in colour, is now largely patinated to milky white. Late 2nd century BC.

35

A gallery in the rock-hewn tomb of the imperial prince Liu Sheng, at Man-ch'eng, Hopei. Pottery vases holding the usual wine offering are seen stacked. Late 2nd century BC.

36 FACING

Bronze wine vase decorated with inlaid gold wire. The arabesques allude to motifs of ancient tradition and incorporate highly ornate and barely legible ideographs, which read: May good fare fill your gate, expand your girth, extend your life, keep sickness at bay. The vase was found in Liu Sheng's tomb. Height 40 cm. 113 BC.

37
Decoration on the side of a bronze drum used as a container for cowries (i.e. money), excavated at the necropolis of the Tien kings of ancient Yünnan. The scene represents a noble female carried in a litter, followed by attendants with hunting cheetahs. About 100 BC. Shih-chai-shan, Yünnan.

38
Bronze trophy of bull heads. On the horns perch complete bulls and the head is framed by snakes. Cattle raising was the basic occupation of the inhabitants of the Tien kingdom, and the bull figures frequently in ornament as it did in religious sacrifice. About 100 BC. Height 11.2 cm. Shih-chai-shan, Yünnan.

40 FACING
Bronze drum adapted as a cowrie container. Hornbills and other birds are a common theme of Tien art, as are such real scenes as the ceremony represented sculpturally on the lid. Women seated at the edge are engaged in weaving, others are offering gifts to the principal, evidently a chieftainess. Height 27.5 cm. About 100 BC. Shih-chai-shan, Yünnan.

39 Bronze plaque of two men dancing. They hold in their hands bronze discs of which the actual examples found in Tien tombs are decorated with shell. The ground line is a snake. Both dancers wear the long iron swords which were the chief weapon of Tien warriors. A contemporary Chinese historian notes that the dancers of south-west China performed with their hands as much as their feet. About 100 BC. Height about 10 cm. Shih-chai-shan, Yünnan.

41

*Isometric drawing of the stone-built funeral chambers of a rich tomb at Yi-nan,
Shantung. The pillars and brackets imitate the shapes of wooden architecture. The
stone walls are largely covered with engraved figures taken from Taoist mythology. The
height of the roof beams above the floor is about 2.5 m. 2nd century AD.*

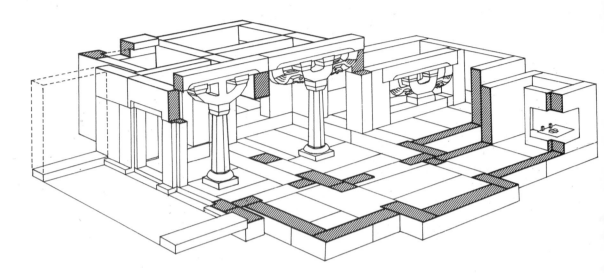

42

*A winged dragon ridden by a winged man, as depicted on the walls of the Yi-nan tomb.
The scene represents a visitation by an emissary of the Taoist paradise in the far west,
where the chief deity, the Queen Mother of the West, lives attended by such winged men
as the one shown here. The details of the scene are not explained. The men holding
sceptres with a cross are perhaps Taoist adepts engaged in calling up immortal spirits.
2nd century AD.*

Wooden carving of a human head with protruding tongue, crowned with deer antlers. This figure comes from a tomb at Ch'ang-sha and appears to be connected with a shamanistic cult. An antlered exorcist is found elsewhere in east Asia, one of his roles being to enter into a trance and so to pass into the realms of immortal spirits. Height 92 cm. 3rd–2nd century BC.

44
*Glazed pottery figures representing men at a game.
The player on the left evidently triumphs after an
adroit move, while his partner is perplexed. Realism
of this order is the rule in the tomb figurines of the
Later Han period. Length of the table 30 cm.
1st–2nd century AD. British Museum.*

45

Bronze wine-warmer with cast relief ornament depicting the magic landscape of Han art. The hills are inhabited by deer, tigers (some of these winged), monkeys and bears. This is the realm of immortal spirits, the various animals denoting the natural powers. Among the latter is the dancing bear Ch'ih-yu, which brandishes weapons in all four paws and symbolises courage. Height about 20 cm. 1st century AD. Freer Gallery of Art.

47
Impressed brick from the walls of a funeral chamber, showing the dance of the creator genies Fu Hsi and Nu Wa. They carry the sun and moon and brandish compass and set-square. Nu Wa, the female of the pair, is on the left; both figures end in dragon tails, which in other representations intertwine. 1st century BC. Yang-tzŭ-shan, Szechwan.

The stone doors opening into an underground burial palace at Yang-tzŭ-shan, Szechwan. The view was taken immediately after the tomb was opened, before its contents had been disturbed. The symbols carved on the door resemble those represented by the bronze mask and ring illustrated in fig. 29, the bird having become a separate item. Tigers and dragons stand for forces of nature, while the fish presumably are the ancient symbol of fertility. 2nd century AD.

48

Impressed brick from the walls of a funeral chamber, showing the entertainers at a feast. These include musicians, dancers and jugglers. At the centre stands the wine bucket. The figure at the lower right is a woman performing the dance of the long sleeves in which she whirls round at great speed. The principal guests are shown at the top left. The increasing distance from the viewer is suggested by placing the figures successively higher in the field, a method characteristic of Han painting. 1st century BC. Szechwan. Yang-tzŭ-shan, Szechwan.

49

Life-size stone lion, probably from the
approach avenue of a great tomb. The
compromise which the sculptor makes
between real and stylised form is typical
of the Han period. Lo Yang Museum.
2nd-3rd century AD.

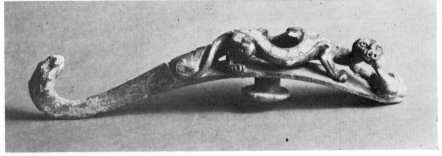

50

Bronze belt hook with a turquoise-inlaid
dragon represented in relief. The dragon's
head is being pushed aside by the arms of
a diminutive monster who only has a
head besides. The bronze is coated with
greenish gold, applied by the amalgam
process. Length 10.2 cm. 1st century
BC. British Museum.

51

Pottery models of farm buildings placed
in Han tombs. One is a sheep stall and
the other shed houses a rotatory rice mill.
1st–2nd century AD. British Museum
and Benaki Museum.

52

Pottery figure of a strange animal combining points of hippopotamus and rhinoceros. This creature appears without precedent in later Han tombs. Its particular meaning is not elucidated. Length about 20 cm. 2nd century AD. Benaki Museum.

53

Bronze model of a horse and carriage from the tomb which contained the flying horse, figure 33. The carriages in the General's procession include one with an umbrella, no doubt intended for himself, and others with emblems, such as an axe, which must denote his chief officers. The horse is of the noble western breed. The harness included a breast band of silk, now decayed, which allowed the horse to take the draught entirely on its shoulders. Height 43.5 cm. 2nd century AD.

54

Segment from the back of a bronze mirror. The relief ornament, taken from Taoist lore, shows celestial dragons biting on the bars of a heavenly structure which joins fixed stars. Among them are figures of Taoist gods and, probably, of the king of the state of Yüeh. 2nd century AD. Former Gure collection.

55

Impression of a mounted archer on a brick from a tomb wall. The horse is posed in the unreal posture of the 'flying leap'. The rider delivers his Parthian shot in true nomad fashion; he rides of course stirrupless. 2nd century AD.

56

Pottery model of a watch-tower from a Han tomb. Han homesteads often look like protected places and usually include a look-out. While much of Han building was entirely in wood it appears from the models that timber bracketing could be combined with brick structures, supporting projecting parts as they do here. 1st–2nd century AD. Height about 45 cm. Benaki Museum.

57

Pottery camel and attendant, glazed in brown and yellow. The camel's load which includes vegetables and game is a fanciful one. The attendant is dressed in the costume of Central Asia and wears a Persian-style beard. The camels placed in tombs around Sian, the T'ang dynasty capital, symbolise the wealth of trade along the Silk Route, as well as the personal distinction of those who benefited from it and employed Central Asian servants. Excavated at Ch'ung-p'u, near Sian, Shensi. Height 47.5 cm. 8th century AD.

5

The T'ang Dynasty

After the fall of the Han dynasty in AD 206 and the fragmentation of the country into smaller hostile states, which the arrival of Buddhist religion did nothing to reconcile, China was not again united until 581, under the Sui emperors. These laid the economic foundation of a stable state, with tentacles reaching out into Central Asia, which the house of T'ang inherited in 618 and built to further heights of prosperity and international prestige.

Many aspects of T'ang civilisation, the classic age of China, are brought together in the sad case of the princess Yung T'ai. Her father, the emperor Chung Tsung, had reigned only a year when his mother, the concubine promoted empress, Wu Tsê T'ien, took power into her own hands. Chung Tsung did not return to the throne until shortly before his mother died in 705, twenty years later.

In 701, when Yung T'ai was nineteen years old and recently married, she was reported to the Empress Wu as having criticised two imperial favourites in a conversation with her husband and her brother-in-law. The position occupied by these young people in the succession was too close for any disloyalty to be tolerated, and the empress ordered all three to take their own lives, or, according to another version in the histories, had them flogged to death. Yung T'ai's father reburied his daughter suitably to her rank immediately after Wu Tsê T'ien's death, although in her epitaph he still took the precaution of attributing her end to childbirth.

In 1964 the Institute of Archaeology of the Academy of Sciences decided to investigate a major royal tomb of the early T'ang period, and following the indication of the histories and local tradition, chose the mound which they believed to be that of the heir apparent Li Hsien, who died in 684. But the tradition was mistaken, and the tomb proved to be that of the princess. This was the first time that any important tomb of the period had been officially opened. It proved different in construction from other royal tombs that had been excavated previously.

The aim of Ch'in and Han emperors had been to build for themselves many-roomed underground palaces, not unlike the residences of their lifetime, but built of stone instead of wood. The greatest of these must be the tomb of the founder of the Ch'in dynasty, whose sheltering mound rises to a height of forty-three metres and is surrounded by a double enclosure measuring 2173 by 974 metres. It has not been violated since it was entered by the Han conqueror of Ch'in. The historian tells us that all the emperor's hundred childless wives were killed and buried with him, as well as the workmen who had been engaged on constructing the tomb; and that among its fabulous treasures is a stone map of China on which the hundred rivers flow with mercury. Later this elaborate style was occasionally imitated, as is seen in the tomb of the first king of the small southern T'ang state of the tenth century. But from the seventh century onwards an imperial tomb seems usually to have taken the form of a long, plain, tunnel-like passage leading to a burial chamber with stone sarcophagus or coffin dais, with some side chambers connecting by long, low entrances. All of this is deep underground, and a high mound faced by an offering chapel covers the region of the burial chamber, the entrance of the access passage being buried and disguised.

This is the shape of Yung T'ai's tomb, but shorn of the side chambers. These are replaced by a series of niches containing over seven hundred marshalled pottery figures of menials. Between the niches the inclined passage of the entrance was joined to the surface by six vertical shafts, subsequently filled in with rammed earth, which were opened to speed the deep digging. One of these shafts had been located by robbers in antiquity, and a narrow tunnel dug down it and along the earth-filled main passage towards the burial chamber and its treasure of gold and silver vessels. Where the robbers' tunnel debouched into the tomb passage lay an iron axe-head and the skeleton of a man who seems to have been one of the gang, or perhaps the unfortunate informer; and silver and glazed pottery were scattered along the passage. The thieves rifled even the high stone sarcophagus in which the remains of the princess and her husband had been placed. But much still remained, and was recovered by the excavators.

The metalwork, pottery and wallpainting which adorned the tomb show Chinese culture on the brink of an age of worldly refinement, with liberal sympathy towards the outside world. During the pre-Sui disunity of the country Chinese influence in central Asia had declined, but now it was restored more completely than before. Along the Silk Route both north and south of the Tarim desert caravans of camels took Chinese weaves to Persia and the Near East, and the return trade brought to China a host of exotic materials and ideas, in art, horticulture, dress, medicine and religion. Zoroastrian temples were allowed to the Persian trading community at the capital, Ch'ang-an, the modern Sian. The effect of these contacts on the upper class around the court reached a climax at the turn of the seventh and eighth centuries. Much of it is reflected in the furnishing of the princess's tomb.

The wall-paintings in the antechamber show two groups of young women dressed in the Persian fashion, with low-cut neck, narrow sleeves and around the shoulders a long stole. The new custom of baring the neck and even riding through the city bareheaded, instead of swathing head and shoulders in an ample veil, shocked sober citizens and delighted poets. Yung T'ai's serving maids carry fans, back-scratchers, boxes with comfits and cosmetics. One of them is dressed in a boy's outfit, still in the Persian style of central Asia.

In the first half of the T'ang period painters were experimenting with the possibility of rendering the rounded form of the human figure by means of long brush lines. Although they were acquainted with a kind of colour-shading, which central Asian painters working in the Indian tradition used to suggest the solidity of natural forms, Chinese masters scorned the super-ficiality of such methods. Their own linear style claimed to interpret three dimensions, and at the same time, through the vigour of the brush stroke, to convey the actual or potential move-ment of living beings. The greatest exponent of the linear style was born about the year of Yung T'ai's death. Wu Tao-tzŭ found a style of figure painting being practised which may be judged to some extent from the tomb paintings, although by comparison with the best of the time these must be journeyman work.

The heyday of the pottery figurines for which the T'ang art is best known outside China today lies also between AD 700 and 750. The large group which was displayed at Yung T'ai's funeral and put to rest with her shows the sculpture fully developed in the characteristic T'ang manner. It con-sists in human *types*, modelled with some psychological insight. The court ladies are shown plausibly vain. Hunts-men concentrate on the matter in hand – one is striking downwards, another is having trouble with an unruly hunt-ing leopard mounted on the crupper of his horse. Many of these menials are given beards, moustaches and large noses and eyes to betoken their central Asian connection. Foreign servants were a mark of distinction, and camels laden with exotic-looking commodi-ties (even vegetables in allusion to the new plants introduced from the west into China) indicated that one was a customer in the doubtless expensive market which they furnished. Animal sculpture based upon close observation of reality had not previously been prominent in Chinese art; but after AD 700 the realism of the noble horse figurines argues close study of the living model, even if the portrayal was always idealised.

When the potter perfected his modelling he also adopted a technique of glazing which had fallen into disuse in China, at least for pottery other than roof tiles, during the previous three centuries. This was lead-fluxed glaze, to which metallic colorants could be added with great effect. At first, before the opening of the T'ang dynasty, only monochrome greens and yellows appear; then suddenly, within a few years of AD 700, browns, greens, blues, yellows blaze into a polychromy which aptly echoes the gay life of the capital as poets and novelists described it. The pottery which has survived was made for placing in tombs. The strong colours covering it repeat the tones and even the designs of fashionable textiles. From central Asia had come a taste for cloth decorated by knot-dyeing and resist-wax dyeing, in which simple units of design blend softly into the ground colour. The general effect is imitated in the famous three-colour variegated wares of T'ang, on which the basic brown, yellow, green and blue are freely splashed and partly overlie each other. This style was transmitted to Japan and to the Near East, and in the latter region founded a long-lasting tradition of ceramic decoration.

When the Arabs invaded Persia in 638 an embassy went to Ch'ang-an to beg the help of the Chinese against the Muslim conquerors. But the Chinese did not care to extend their commitment beyond the Pamir, and refused to send troops. Eventually the son of the last Persian king came to the Chinese capital as a refugee and settled there. Very direct evidence of Persian contacts is seen in T'ang silver and gold, some wine-cups copying Persian models quite closely. Yet the majority of work executed in gold and silver is clearly of Chinese invention, although it breaks with decorative styles of the preceding periods. The designs are chased (made with an instrument which grooves the surface of the metal without cutting it). Wine-cups and ewers are the commonest shapes, and floral scrolls based upon a lotus bloom the most popular motif of the ornament. The lotus, symbol of the Buddha, is ubiquitous in T'ang art.

The largest and finest treasure of gold and silver found in recent times was excavated in 1970, on the site of a mansion at the T'ang capital which records show to have belonged to a cousin of the emperor. This Prince of Pin died in AD 741, and the burial of more than a thousand pieces of gold and silver in two large jars in his garden or beneath his house suggests more than ordinary caution. In 756 the rebellion of An Lu-shan obliged the emperor and court to flee from Ch'ang-an temporarily, and it is probably during this emergency that the treasure was hidden. Included with the silver were Persian, Byzantine and Japanese coins – so widely ranged the trade of which Ch'ang-an was the centre. With the rebellion is associated the saddest story in the personal annals of Chinese emperors. In order to persuade his army to remain loyal, Hsüan Tsung was compelled to allow the death of his favourite concubine Yang Kuei-fei, whose previous favours to the rebel himself put her under suspicion of treason when the trouble broke out. Afterwards Chinese poets never tired of singing the fate of her 'whose smiles awaked a thousand beauties', and who from Paradise sent a message of enduring love to a broken-hearted emperor.

Both the secular and the Buddhist art of the T'ang period had an influence far beyond the borders of China. The linear painting style became the accepted manner in icons of Buddhas and Bodhisattvas in most of the oasis cities of central Asia, beginning with the great emporium of Turfan just beyond the Jade Gate which marked the exit westwards from China. The glories of the Buddhist temples built in Nara, the Japanese capital, during the first half of the eighth century, are the creation of emigrant Chinese artists. In the far west (Persia and the other countries of the Near East), the Chinese were held to be most remarkable for their figured silks. Fortunately the warm sand of such stations on the Silk Route as Turfan and Min-feng have preserved fragments of the weaves from which we can appreciate the artistry of colour and design as well as the barely credible skill of the weaving technique. Recent excavations have recovered specimens which range in date from the Han to the T'ang. Already at the beginning of this span of time a five-coloured silk damask could be woven with a pattern for which seventy-five selections of the warps were needed. Gauzes, with twisted warps, were woven from the Han period onwards. An elaborate flowered stuff could use eight colours and double warps. These silks were the wonder of the medieval western world, and it is understandable that they launched a legend of the skill of Chinese craftsmen which has lasted to our own day.

Fifteen years after An Lu-shan rebelled the old splendid life had departed from Ch'ang-an for good. Nor did the easy cosmopolitanism survive. The pretty coloured pottery ceased, or was much simplified, and the fine art of the silversmith declined. Soon a Tibetan occupation of the north-west threatened the trade passing along the Silk Route and temporarily impeded the cultural flow. But what ensued was the twilight of a comparatively small and privileged community centred on the capital. China as a whole gathered new energies, and in many ways her greatest time was still to come.

Stele of white marble representing the Buddha Śākyamuni under Śāla trees, between disciples and Bodhisattvas. The Buddhist religion, having spread increasingly in China from the 4th century AD, achieved under the T'ang dynasty the greatest wealth and eminence. Its images followed models which can be traced back to India and Central Asia, but the style of the carving is Chinese. The Buddha, enthroned under the trees where he reached Enlightenment, is a frequent theme. At the base of the carving lions and guardians in human form flank the sacred jewel which denotes the Buddha and his message. Excavated at Lin-chang, Hopei. Height 72.6 cm. Mid-6th century AD.

59
The idea of the spiritual guardian of the tomb was very ancient in China, and in the T'ang dynasty coincided sculpturally with the guardians of the Buddhist religion and of the state. This figure in stoneware, with cream and brown glaze, was excavated from the tomb of a general at Anyang, Honan. The military costume still includes the leather helmet of the northern warriors. Height 64 cm. AD 595.

VIII

Stoneware jar decorated with two phoenixes. The design is executed in black slip on which incised lines are cut through to the clay body. The ground is also a white slip. This outstanding piece of tzu-chou ware was found in a forgotten storehouse below ground at Liang-hsiang, near Peking. Height 36 cm. Yüan dynasty AD 1271–1368.

See pp. 101 ff.

IX

An eight-faceted porcelain vase decorated with dragons and waves in underglaze blue. The bodies of the dragons are raised in low relief and incised to show scales. The fan-shaped figures at the foot and on the shoulders are filled with floral motifs. The whole compact ornament is characteristic of Yüan taste. Found in a hoard of porcelain buried at Pao-ting, Hopei. Height 51.5 cm. 14th century AD.

See pp. 101 ff.

60

Fragment of five-coloured silk damask
found near Turfan, Sinkiang. This
piece came from a tomb dated AD
551, and indicates the revival of trade
along the Silk Route through Central
Asia, which took place in the mid-6th
century. Its decoration is archaic, con-
trasting with the more natural animal
and floral designs which were due
shortly to be introduced.

61

Fragment of eight-colour silk damask with birds and flowers, from
a tomb dated AD 778 at Turfan, Sinkiang. This decorative style
is characteristic of much of the finest craft produced at the T'ang
capital. The weave has double warps and a density of 32 threads to
the centimetre. Among the flowers appear phoenixes and the
magic fungus.

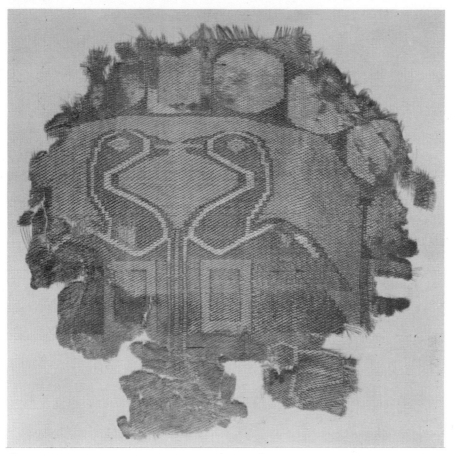

62

Fragment of silk damask with confronted ducks in a beaded frame, found in a grave at Turfan, Sinkiang, dated AD 668. The heraldic style and the beaded frame are characteristic of Persian or Central Asian rather than Chinese style.

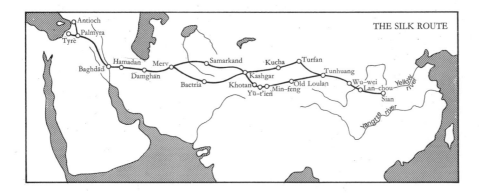

63

The Silk Route. The bulk of the T'ang trade passed along the northern branch through Central Asia, by Turfan, Kucha and Kashgar.

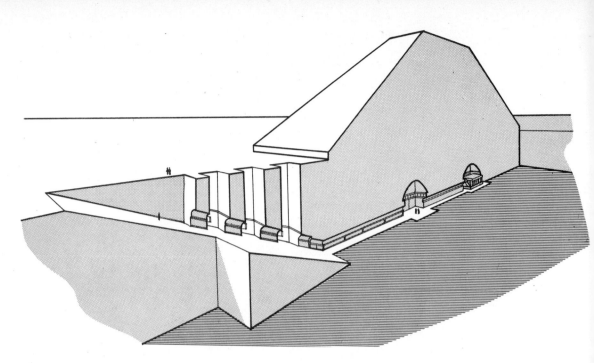

64

Cutaway drawing of the tomb of Prince Chang Huai who died in AD 684. The scale may be judged from the figures shown standing in the ante-chamber. The burial chamber with sarcophagus is approximately under the middle of the mound which marks the tomb on the surface. The shafts rising vertically from the sloping entrance helped in the construction of the tomb. The tomb of the Princess Yung T'ai followed the same design and scale.

65 FACING

Pottery figure of a mounted huntsman, glazed green and brown, from the tomb of the Princess Yung T'ai at Ch'ien-hsien, Shensi. The rider seems to be controlling a hunting cheetah which he probably carried on the crupper of his horse. Height 31 cm. About AD 700.

66 LEFT

Glazed pottery figure of the protective genie Ch'i-t'ou from a tomb at Ch'ung-p'u, Shensi, of the early 8th century AD. The grotesque human head is placed on an animal's body, the horn, large ears and flaming shoulders denoting his powers directed against evil spirits. Height 57.5 cm.

67

Silver cup with chased decoration of a huntsman galloping through a blossoming landscape. The shape of the cup is derived from Persian silverware, the leafed scroll around the lip is a frequent motif in T'ang decoration. Such silver craft flourished during the first half of the 8th century AD. Height about 12 cm.

68

A 'winged cup' of parcel gilt silver with chased ornament of peony scrolls and a sacred duck, the Indian hamsa, standing on a lotus pedestal. The shape copies a fashion of the Han period, when cups were made of lacquered wood. Peony-fancying was a rage at the T'ang capital, and the flower dominates in ornament. The duck is an element of western exoticism such as the T'ang patron loved. This piece belonged to a large treasure of gold and silver apparently abandoned at Sian when the imperial capital was occupied by rebels in AD 756. Height 2.8 cm.

69, 70, 71

Three pieces from the treasure found at Ho-chia, respectively in gold, silver gilt, silver. The gold bowl, with its sides shaped into lotus petals, is decorated with the scatter of animals and flowers that was recognised by the patrons of T'ang craft as the western Persian style. As in all such pieces, the work is executed by a chaser, which grooves the metal without cutting it, and a punch. The silver gilt cup with a ring handle follows a Persian form exactly. The relief figures are musicians holding instruments or attendants with cups, standing against a ground of characteristic T'ang floral scrolling. The silver platter with badgers is one of a number in which lively and fairly realistic figures of animals are designed in repoussé. Height respectively 5.5 cm, 6.5 cm, 22.5 cm. Mid-8th century AD.

72

Stoneware jug with light and dark brown glaze. The applied decorative panels show a bird, a lion and a floral medallion. Excavated near Ch'ang-sha, Hunan. Height 22.5 cm. 9th century AD.

73

Pottery bowl glazed brown, yellow and green from the tomb of the Princess Yung T'ai. The shape approximates to that of a silver bowl but the dappled lead-glazed decoration more resembles knot-dyed textile. Height 7.4 cm. About AD 700.

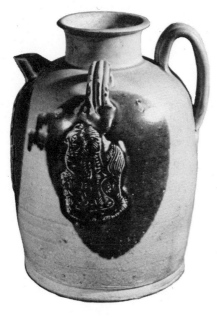

74

Pottery ewer decorated in three-colour glaze. The ewer with a hawk-head neck certainly was elaborated originally in metal. It was a popular form of the highly decorative ceramic product of the T'ang potter during the first half of the 8th century AD. Height 32.2 cm. Found at Loyang, Honan.

75

Tripod, ting, *in celadon porcelain, as made at the Yao-hsien kilns in Shensi. At this centre were produced one of the finest wares of the Northern Sung period, between c. 1050 and 1127, the so-called northern celadon. Some pieces reflect the interest in ancient ritual and its bronze appurtenances which arose at the end of the 11th century. This tripod imitates, but in a much altered version, the shape and decoration of the ancient sacrificial vessel. Excavated at Lan-t'ien, Shensi. Height 57 cm.*

6

The Sung Dynasty

The Sung period divides at the year 1127, when the tribes of the Jurchen invaded north China and founded their Chin dynasty. The court fled from the capital at K'ai-feng in Honan, leaving the emperor Hui Tsung, famous as painter and aesthete, in the enemy's hands. Hui Tsung's brother established a government at Hangchow, south of the Yangtze mouth, and the Sung house continued to rule until its extinction by the Mongol invaders in 1279.

In art the Sung dynasty is equally celebrated as the golden age of Chinese landscape-painting and as the time which saw the potter's art brought to a perfection which has never been surpassed. The two movements are related only through the imperial patronage which they both received: painting by the founding of an academy by Hui Tsung, which was revived after the flight south, and porcelain by the creation of an imperial factory at Hangchow. Aesthetically the two arts diverge. Painting begins in a mood of robust romanticism and ends under the southern Sung in stereotyped sentimentality. The lonely fishermen on misty waters under wet beetling cliffs, in which the poetic southern Sung painter delighted, were the approximate equivalent of the Monarch of the Glen looming out of the rain to which Victorian Englishmen were addicted. In porcelain the imperial influence was towards purity of form – the potter often being required to imitate the noble simplicity of ancient ritual vessels – and towards excellence in monochrome glaze, intended to capture the deep lustre of jade.

Recently the archaeologist has furnished an early chapter in the history of hard-glazed ceramics in China. Currently the excavation of kiln sites adds yearly to knowledge of the technical and commercial basis of the craft in which the Chinese were – and still are – the unsurpassed masters.

From the neolithic age Shang potters of 1500 BC inherited an unusually efficient type of kiln, in which the separation of stoking chamber from kilning chamber by a more or less horizontal flue ensured a good draught and a clean flame. This kiln had enabled the Yangshao potters to maintain a uniform tone in their red ceramic and to fire to near-stoneware hardness. Moreover, their bronze-age successors stumbled on two prime discoveries without realising their potentiality: pure white clay, *kaolin*, which they used for rather clumsy thick-sided pots on which the ornament was carved in imitation of the designs used on bronze; and the art of investing hard-baked clay with a coating of glass, or glazed pottery. Together these two discoveries anticipated the invention of porcelain three thousand years later.

Egypt had known glazed pottery at an even earlier date than its appearance in China. This glaze was based on alkali (potash or soda) and did not adhere well to clay (being therefore mostly used on a non-clay body). The Chinese invention however was a glaze with very little alkali in it, consisting largely of silica, which united strongly with the surface of the pot. Such *hard* glaze demands a kiln temperature in the region of 1200° C. The announcement of this Chinese achievement was at first met with scepticism, and it was suggested that the glaze had formed accidentally in the kiln through contact with wood ash. But the separation of the stoking chamber of the kiln from the pottery makes this unlikely, and the uniform thickness and colour of the coating point to deliberate glazing.

After the Shang period *kaolin* seems to have been abandoned as unsuitable for making pottery on the wheel, or even for making thin-walled vessels by hand. Shang potters used their glaze on only two or three undistinguished shapes with sides marked with twisted cords or stamped with a criss-cross of lines. The reason for such a limited application of the new technique has not been explained. The advantage of being waterproof was obtained by the high-temperature firing even without glaze, and in competition with other kinds of decoration the latter was perhaps not much prized.

Hard glazing is traced sporadically until the end of the first century BC, when it was brought into regular production. Meantime an alternative *soft* glaze, consisting of silica combined with a comparatively large amount of lead oxide, had made a rather mysterious appearance. The use of lead in glaze had also been known to the Egyptians at a much earlier time and in various stages of development, but in China its adoption in the Han dynasty was not preceded by any experimental phase. It is therefore difficult to refute the argument that lead-glazing, like the manufacture of lead-fluxed glass itself, may have been an import into China from the Near East, where it was known from about the third century BC. The most imaginative exploitation of lead glaze is seen in the first half of the eighth century, in the polychrome pots and figurines which are an important element of the exotic Persianising art of T'ang capital.

For the Chinese the distinction made in the west between porcelain and stoneware does not exist, both being denoted *tz'ŭ*. In the west porcelain is described as a dense ware that rings with a clear note when struck, and in thin section is slightly translucent with a pinkish colour. In stoneware the particles of clay, being less closely fused together, transmit less light, but it is no less waterproof than porcelain.

The gradual improvement which led to porcelain took place initially in the region of the Yangtze delta, in the south of Kiangsu and the north of Chekiang, where unglazed ware of stoneware quality had been made since the third century BC. First came the Han dynasty vases with brown-green and slightly dappled feldspathic glaze, and these were replaced in the latter half of the third century BC by a green-surfaced ware, the ancestor of celadons, which owed its colour to iron oxide added to the glaze. By the T'ang period the beauty of this *Yüeh* ware (so named after the ancient kingdom established in the region) was a by-word with poets, and three centuries later the celadons of the Lung-ch'üan kilns of Chekiang reached a perfection that was never recaptured in later times. The glaze is praised by contemporaries for its deep glow (as opposed to a vulgar glassiness) which allied it to jade, an effect produced by careful control of the size and density of minute bubbles induced in the interior of the glaze during firing.

The trial of clays which led to the formulation of the perfected porcelain body went on both in Kiangsu-Chekiang and, in the north, Honan and especially Hopei. The problem was to find a means of rendering pure *kaolin*, the 'china clay' which had been known since Shang times, sufficiently fusible to produce a dense body, in which the particles are cemented together. This was done by adding to the *kaolin* a quantity of crushed feldspar, i.e. the very mineral whose decay in the earth had produced the *kaolin* itself.

In north and south China porcelain was produced to this formula, and decorated with coloured glazes that set fashions for certain districts. In Shensi the Yao-chou kilns vied with those of Lung-ch'üan in Chekiang in producing celadons. Hopei in the north-east specialised in white porcelain from the late T'ang dynasty onwards, and at various kilns in the south black glazes, and the decorative glazes called 'hare's fur' and 'oil spot' were used on tea bowls. At the 'imperial' kilns near Hangchow and at Lung-ch'üan particular attention was paid to effects which imitated jade and ancient bronze. One device was the control of crackle in the glaze by adjusting differences in shrinkage between glaze and body. It was possible to produce crackle of different grades, a fine crazing within a broad mesh.

After the Sung period only three major technical developments in the art of porcelain remained to be mastered. These were underglaze painting, which was introduced in the Yüan period; overglaze enamelling, which flourished in the floral and figural ornament of Ming wares; and the enrichment of glaze colour by new metallic colorants, of which copper proved the most interesting by its production of greens and reds. By the eighteenth century nearly every colour of the spectrum could be given to glaze, and the subtlety of enamel glazes painted over the hard glaze vied with the painter's palette.

Isometric drawing of the funeral chambers in the tomb of the Emperor Li Pien of the Southern T'ang dynasty, built about AD 950. Since they have not been excavated, the structure of the tombs of the Sung emperors is not known, but it is likely that they follow the practice of the 10th century as it is seen here. The pillars, cornices and brackets of Li Pien's tomb were painted largely with floral scrolls of the kind common in T'ang art and used on the earlier Sung porcelain. The platform in the rear chamber supported the sarcophagus. The stonework imitates a wooden building, in the manner of the Han tomb shown in figure 41. Total length 21.5 m.

76

Porcelain ewer and bowl for warming wine, with light blue ch'ing-pai glaze. The allusion to the lotus in the lobes of the bowl and the petals at its foot shows the Sung inheritance of the pervasive T'ang motif. The handle, neck and spout of the ewer appear to copy a metal prototype. Excavated at Tê-an, Kiangsi. Height of the ewer, 25.8 cm. 12th or 13th century AD.

78

The entrance to the inner chamber of the Emperor Li Pien's tomb, showing it as it was just after the brick sealing had been broken. The guardian figures wear parade armour. On the lintel two feline dragons flank a flaming pearl: this motif was per-petuated as a symbol of the imperial dignity. The brick corbelling of the roof repeats the technique, known in China from the Han period.

79

View across the first court of the Imperial Palace, Peking, showing the approach to the first audience hall, T'ai-ho-tien (Hall of Universal Peace). The white marble bridges and palisades and the buildings them-selves date from the Ming reconstruction of the palace completed early in the 15th century AD, but in general the plan of Kublai's palace is reproduced.

7

The Yüan Dynasty

The Yüan, or Mongol, dynasty of China holds a special interest for the West. It was in this period that the first Europeans entered China. In 1271 the Genoese merchant brothers Marco, Matteo and Niccolo Polo set out on their second journey to the Far East. They had already been at the Great Khan's court in Peking, whence they had returned with his suggestion that 'a hundred men learned in the Christian religion' might visit his empire. The Polos left accompanied by only two unenthusiastic friars, who never reached the destination, but with the blessing of Pope Gregory X.

At this time commercial interest and political caution, as well as romantic curiosity, impelled Europeans towards contacts with the Mongol conquerors of Asia. The alliance of cattle-herding plainsmen of inner Asia, founded by Genghis Khan at Karakorum in eastern Mongolia in 1206, had by the Polos' time subjugated the whole of the inhabitable continent except Europe, Arabia and some distant archipelagos. Christians trembled, but were content to watch 'dog eat dog' as the Muslims fell victims to the invaders. The defeat of national states and overriding of religious barriers opened up Central Asia to travellers and trade. China for the first time found herself incorporated into a political unit embracing western peoples. Of the merchants who took advantage of this *pax mongolica* Marco Polo is the only one to have left a record of his experiences, his sober observation of the Chinese scene throwing a light on affairs which is missing from the native histories.

Next to Genghis, the name of his grandson Kublai is the most familiar to the West. When the Polos arrived in China in 1272 he had only just completed his conquest of the Sung empire of south China, but had already been long enough in possession of the north to have largely completed the building of his two capitals. The upper one, Shang-tu (Coleridge takes one of Polo's spellings, Xanadu) was situated a short distance north of Peking, beyond the Great Wall. Here he built a marble palace 'marvellously embellished', which abutted on to a wall encircling sixteen miles of hunting park. Kublai would often enter this enclosure with a cheetah on the crupper of his horse. The remains of the stately pleasure dome still await the attention of the archaeologist. It is the great palace he built in Peking, Ta-tu, the great capital, of which some features have been recently excavated.

Peking, known as Khan-balik (the Lord's City), was Kublai's creation. He followed Chinese precedent in adopting square precincts both for the outer limiting wall and the two inner walls surrounding the palace, which was his residence and the seat of government. All were orientated to the four cardinal directions, for the Khan, assisted by his numerous astrologers, would not treat lightly the Chinese practice regarding location and direction. The palace faced the principal gateway in the south wall. The outermost wall, according to Marco, had a total length of twenty-four miles, which proves to be nearer to eighteen. In each of its sides, he says, were three gateways with towers surrounding them (in fact there were only two in the north wall), and a further three towers at the corners, all of these sheltering soldiers and serving as arsenals. The gates opened on to straight roads crossing the city and dividing it into rectangular sections. In theory the whole population was to be contained within the perimeter, but Marco tells us how there were already suburbs overflowing at the gateways.

Towards the middle of the city so defined stood the palace precinct, both of the walls encircling it having eight defensive towers. Of gateways there were five in the southern walls and one in each side of the remaining walls. Between the walls two extensive ponds were dug and stocked with fish, which were prevented by iron grills from escaping into the ever-flowing stream that passed through. A long mound raised with the spoil from these excavations was planted with many varieties of trees, even fully grown ones being transplanted, and grass was sown in the great courtyard to remind the Khan of the vast spaces of the steppe plains where nomadic virtue and liberty reigned.

Kublai's city has suffered alteration since his time, but the chequer-board plan was for long respected. Much of the outermost wall has been removed

(some of it in the last few years) and it is commemorated at places only by street names. What baffles the archaeologist in attempting to recover the plan of the Yüan palace is the fact that when the Ming emperors rebuilt and extended it in the early fifteenth and the eighteenth centuries, the old plan was largely adhered to. We are entitled to assume that the general appearance of the palace, the Forbidden City, as it stands today, does not depart over-much from the sight that met the eyes of the astonished Genoese in 1272. In details many features have undoubtedly changed; but the effect will have remained much the same: noble roofs resplendent in coloured tiles, hipped and curving at the eaves; large expanses of courtyard between the carved marble sides of the foundation platforms on which the principal buildings stood; and the lateral galleries with their rows of smaller latticed rooms. Marco notes that the palace had no upper floors, and that the 'basement on which it stands is raised ten palms above the level of the surrounding earth', which is about the height of much of it today. He was greatly moved by the 'halls and chambers . . . covered with gold and silver and decorated with pictures of dragons and birds and horsemen and various breeds of beasts and scenes of battle' (tr. R. E. Latham, Penguin).

The renovation of the palace was undertaken by the third Ming emperor, beginning shortly after 1403. The perimeters on north and south were moved farther south, and those on east and west were retained. In 1969 and 1970 the demolition of parts of the Ming and Ch'ing dynasty walls gave archaeologists their chance. In the middle of the west wall the Gate of Peace and Justice, which still stands with the original Yüan brickwork, was cleared, and within its entrance were excavated the greater part of the foundations of residential pavilions and courtyards of the same date. These are identified as the Ho-ying-fang (The Residence of Later Blossom) from a neighbouring street preserving the name. What has been revealed of the foundations covers forty metres from east to west and twenty-five from north to south. The main feature is a hall measuring fifteen by twelve metres, with four central and twelve side pillars. At one place a low platform (a 'moon platform', *yüeh-t'ai*) projects into a courtyard, and is approached by steps leading between two stone lions. Although the regular merchants' quarters of the city were far from the palace, one may still imagine the Ho-ying-fang to be a place where guests entering by the Peace and Justice Gate might be received; and even picture the Polos, at some moment of their twenty-year-long residence in the city, passing between the lions on to the privileged elevation of the *yüeh-t'ai*.

The excavators were surprised to find so much debris of massive glass and thickly glazed earthenware, all of which had evidently belonged to the buildings. A rather garish display of colour is what one would expect at Kublai's court, judging from new styles of pottery ornament which became fashionable under the Mongols. To Marco's medieval eye the lavish colour of buildings would not come amiss. It does not occur to him to censure what he sees for excessive ostentation or extravagance. The fine paving-stone of the rooms, the marble pillar-footings and the trace of latticed doors give an idea of elegant if not necessarily comfortable living. The elegance of the palace furnishings is best judged from the fragments of porcelain and lacquer vessels which were found on and near the site. Some of the lacquer is inlaid with mother-of-pearl, and pieces of both materials are inscribed with the words 'palace' (*nei fu*) or 'palace general use'.

The most remarkable advance made in craft during the Yüan period is seen in the porcelains, particularly in the introduction towards the end of the dynasty of painting in blue pigment. This depended on the employment of a cobalt mineral (asbolite or cobalite) which at first had to be imported from the Near East, and hence became known in China as Muhammedan blue. The pigment is painted on to the white body of the unfired porcelain, then covered with the glazing material and placed in the kiln. After firing, when the glaze has fused indivisibly with the clay of the body, the particles of blue are found suspended within the glaze. By this means the potter was able to paint decoration almost as freely as an artist using brush and paper. The earliest dated pieces on which it was employed are two vases in the Percival David Foundation of Chinese Art in London, whose inscription places their manufacture in the year 1351. By then the method is so accomplished that we must suppose it to have been practised for some time past. Gradually the blue was refined to a pure sapphire tone which, combined with the pure white of the porcelain ground, produced one of the most striking effects ever achieved in ceramics. The invention, which may have reached China from Persia, came after the Polos' time, or they could hardly have failed to notice it. Almost at once blue-and-white porcelain became important in trade with the Near East, where many early specimens still survive, and whence many have come to Europe. By the mid-sixteenth century vases and plates painted with flowers, landscape and figures were commanding high prices in Europe, and efforts to reproduce their technique were made in most European countries. The result was the foundation in the course of the seventeenth century of the western tradition of blue-painted glazed earthenware which is variously known as Delft or Lambeth. These in turn were the progenitors of a host of modern utilitarian wares decorated with blue upon white, whose ancestors are porcelains once set before the Mongol emperors of China.

80 FACING

The Gate of Peace and Justice in the middle of the west wall of Kublai's palace perimeter. The massive brickwork suggests walls of greater height and breadth than the present ones, and designed with more concern for military defence. This is one of the few surviving fragments of the original Yüan fabric.

81

Foundations, as excavated, of the Hou-ying-fang (Residence of Later Blossom). The stone platforms were the floors of the pillared wooden buildings raised on them. The detail of paths, steps and recesses is unusually elaborate.

82

The Hou-ying-fang in the course of excavation.

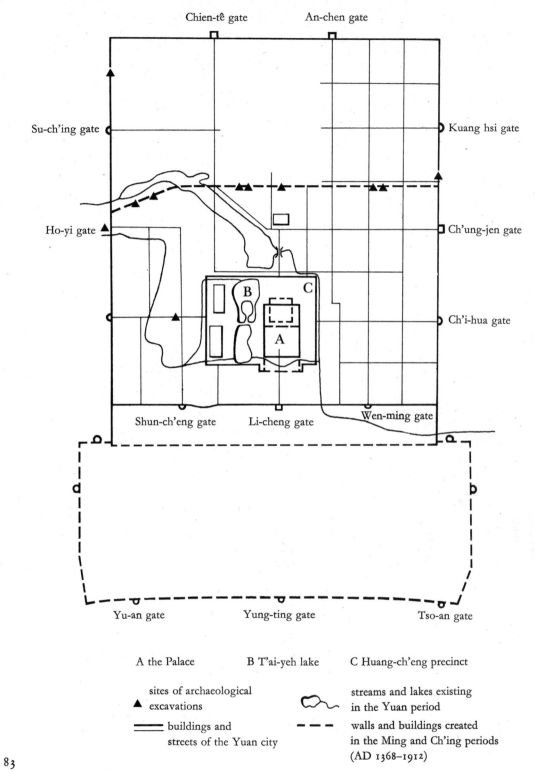

Chien-tê gate   An-chen gate

Su-ch'ing gate   Kuang hsi gate

Ho-yi gate   Ch'ung-jen gate

B   C

A   Ch'i-hua gate

Shun-ch'eng gate   Li-cheng gate   Wen-ming gate

Yu-an gate   Yung-ting gate   Tso-an gate

A the Palace   B T'ai-yeh lake   C Huang-ch'eng precinct

▲ sites of archaeological excavations

⌇ streams and lakes existing in the Yuan period

─── buildings and streets of the Yuan city

- - - walls and buildings created in the Ming and Ch'ing periods (AD 1368–1912)

83

Plan of the Imperial City and Palace in Khan-balik (Peking).
eighteen miles. The circumference of the Yüan walls is about

84

In the shapes of porcelain the chief innovation of the Yüan potter was the copying of bronze forms of Near Eastern design, such as this wine ewer. The underglaze-blue painting of the 14th century, with its spots and irregularities, is technically inferior to that executed from the 15th century onwards, but is full of fresh vigour savouring little of the pattern book. This is one of a number of fine porcelains discovered intact in an underground store-room at Pao-ting, Hopei. Height 26.5 cm. Mid-14th century AD.

85

Ritual goblet, ku, in white porcelain with underglaze-blue decoration. Under the Yüan emperors there was a marked increase in the production of porcelain and bronze vessels imitating the ancient ritual pieces. Excavated at Peking. Height 13.3 cm. Mid-14th century AD.